"Stan Gale's goal in 7... ple expression of fait... in plain, biblical language. He succeeds admirably in a book that is wise, clear, and pastoral. The exposition of the Creed is grounded in Scripture and is theologically rich. With winsome illustrations from various walks of life, it will be edifying for believers and winsome for seekers."

—Dan Doriani, professor of theology, Covenant Seminary

"These are the words of a seasoned minister who knows personally and pastorally the enduring value of this historic creed. Stan delivers crisp and insightful theological exposition, yet his warm, witty, and colorful prose will keep you glued to your seat. And then, whether young catechumen or seasoned saint, you will leap to your feet to confess your faith more passionately than ever before. Routine will give way to robust proclamation!"

—David B. Garner, associate professor of systematic theology and vice president for advancement, Westminster Theological Seminary, Philadelphia

"As Stan Gale explains, the Apostles' Creed gives us a form and framework for declaring and growing in our faith. This ancient standard, familiar to many Christians yet unknown by most, holds the key to a right focus in worship and an expansive walk in the life of faith. Like a docent in an art museum, Stan walks us point by point through the rich textures and spiritual colors of the Creed, expanding on each phrase with sound biblical instruction and typical 'Gale-ic' illustrations from everyday life. Read this book, then read it again reflectively. Not only will you understand the Creed as never before but you'll find your worship of God greatly enhanced and illuminated and your walk with Jesus more a source of confidence and joy than you've ever known."

—T. M. Moore, author and principal of The Fellowship of Ailbe

"Pastor Stan Gale has given us a study of the Apostles' Creed that is set in the world in which most of us live. He has done a real service to the church by expounding this most basic of all statements of Christian belief. Expect some fresh insights and ample scriptural support for this essential tool of Christian discipleship."

—Stephen Smallman, author of *Understanding the Faith*

THE
CHRISTIAN'S
Creed

Other Reformation Heritage Books publications by Stanley D. Gale

- *A Vine-Ripened Life: Spiritual Fruitfulness through Abiding in Christ*
- *Why Must We Forgive?*
  (Cultivating Biblical Godliness series)
- *Finding Forgiveness: Discovering the Healing Power of the Gospel*

THE CHRISTIAN'S Creed

EMBRACING THE APOSTOLIC FAITH

Stanley D. Gale

Reformation Heritage Books
Grand Rapids, Michigan

Reformation Heritage Books
2965 Leonard St. NE
Grand Rapids, MI 49525
616–977–0889
orders@heritagebooks.org
www.heritagebooks.org

Printed in the United States of America
18 19 20 21 22 23/10 9 8 7 6 5 4 3 2 1

Library of Congress Control Number: 2018942460

ISBN: 978-1-60178-617-3 (paperback)
ISBN: 978-1-60178-618-0 (epub)

For additional Reformed literature, request a free book list from Reformation Heritage Books at the above regular or email address.

To
Glenn Evans, Dwight Dunn,
and Darin Pesnell,

brothers in the Lord, partners in the gospel

Contents

Acknowledgments

"Were there not ten cleansed? But where are the nine? Were there not any found who returned to give glory to God?" (Luke 17:17–18). Ten lepers had cried out to Jesus for mercy. He heard their plea and granted their petition. The rest of the story tells us that only one of the ten returned to give Him thanks. In that spirit, I begin my acknowledgments with gratitude to God—Father, Son, and Holy Spirit—for His many answers to prayer in the writing of this book. His work to help me organize my thoughts, bring to mind the scope of His revelation in the Scriptures, and find words to express rich truths made the writing experience a delight. My continuing prayer is that He would use this volume to incite others to follow in the footsteps of the cleansed leper and give praise to God for grace, power, and healing.

In addition to recognizing the work of God in my writing this book and as the One whose teaching undergirds the declarations of the Apostles' Creed, I want to express appreciation for those fellow humans who contributed to it, beginning with Joel Beeke, Jay Collier, and Annette Gysen of Reformation Heritage Books. I am humbled by their support of my writing endeavors and blessed by their expertise in publishing. I am grateful to my writer's group—Alexandra, Gretchen, Audra, and Stephen—for their technical insights and stimulating interactions. My wife, Linda, is not a part of the writing, but she is an integral part of the writer. In her I have found a good thing. She is indeed an excellent wife, in whom I have found favor from the Lord (Prov. 18:22).

The Apostles' Creed

I believe in God, the Father almighty,
  Maker of heaven and earth.

I believe in Jesus Christ, his only Son, our Lord,
  who was conceived by the Holy Spirit
  and born of the virgin Mary.
  He suffered under Pontius Pilate,
  was crucified, died, and was buried;
  he descended to hell.
  The third day he rose again from the dead.
  He ascended to heaven
  and is seated at the right hand of
    God the Father almighty.
  From there he will come to judge the
    living and the dead.

I believe in the Holy Spirit,
  the holy catholic church,
  the communion of saints,
  the forgiveness of sins,
  the resurrection of the body,
  and the life everlasting. Amen.

Introduction
CONFESSING THE FAITH

I sat across from a fellow pastor over the lunch table. "I just wish they would give a simple expression of faith," the pastor said. He was relating to me his experience of interviewing youth for church membership and lamenting their efforts to impress him by punctuating their testimony with words like *justification* and *vicarious*. My friend went on, "I would love to hear them recite the Apostles' Creed to tell me what they believe."

Certainly that simple statement of faith my friend was looking for finds no better expression than the Apostles' Creed. The Creed dates to the early days of the Christian church, its original form tracing to the second century and the present version to the sixth century. It is attributed to the apostles not because they directly wrote it but because it reflects apostolic doctrine, the inspired teaching God gave to the apostles and prophets upon which His church is built (cf. Eph. 2:20; 4:4–6).

The apostles, of course, wrote much more than what is contained in the Creed. While the Creed summarizes apostolic teaching, it does not exhaust it. In fact, the Apostles' Creed seems to focus on one particular aspect of their teaching, the gospel of Jesus Christ, which unfolds in Trinitarian fullness—Father, Son, and Holy Spirit. The Creed is markedly Christian, holding forth the only God in His trinity. The emphasis, though, is not God in His eternal being but God in His redeeming work. It lays out a redemption rooted in the eternal Father who appointed salvation, the incarnate Son who accomplished salvation, and the given Spirit who applies salvation. Its intent is not as much to teach about the unrivaled God as it is to display the unfurling of the gospel in a God-centered salvation.

As a creed, it serves as a statement of belief. The word *creed* originates from the Latin *credere*, meaning to believe or to entrust. The Apostles' Creed communicates fundamentals of the faith. It is authoritative, in one sense, by its universal recognition but primarily because it derives from the Bible, the word of God Himself. While the Apostles' Creed does not seem to have risen out of doctrinal conflict or have been issued by a church council, as was the case with the Nicene Creed, it has been acknowledged over the years to affirm biblical teaching. It has found use since the early church in initiating someone into the Christian faith and affirming that faith.

By the Apostles' Creed we make a confession of faith. *Confess* in the Greek (*homologeo*) means "to say the same thing." *Homo* means same; *logeo*, to speak. When we confess our sins, we say the same thing as God. Such confession admits wrong and adopts God's assessment. In embracing the Creed, we align ourselves with its teaching and God's revelation of Himself and declaration of truth in the Bible. In that sense, we not only believe in God but we believe God. We agree with what He says and embrace that revelation as our own. When we embrace the Creed as our own through faith, we speak loyalty to the One before whom we make the declarations in it. In that sense, it is a pledge of allegiance for Christ's church, an expression of submission and devotion to His redemptive kingdom. Its scope reaches to eternity past and stretches to eternity future, where the confessing believer sees his or her name etched by the gracious hand of God.

Although the "I believe" that initiates the Creed expresses *personal* faith, the Creed serves as a rallying point for the *community* of faith. That's why its recitation fits well in corporate worship. The echoes of "I believe" fill the room as those Christians gathered for worship join in chorus to say, "I believe with you." Together we declare in the hearing of the One we have gathered to worship, "We believe," to the glory of God, whose grace is manifest in hearts enabled by the Holy Spirit. The Creed puts words to worship.

The Apostles' Creed serves a dual function. While it gives declarations to *believers* to help them express their faith, the same words give statements to searching *unbelievers* to help them encounter the faith. It answers the question, What must I sincerely believe in order to be a disciple of Jesus Christ? While Christian denominations feature their own emphases and nuances, the Creed spells out the core, the basics of the faith, the beating heart of the gospel. A person cannot consider himself or herself a Christian apart from a sincere embrace of the tenets laid out in the Creed. For that reason, a study of the Creed provides a lesson plan of life, leading to "the life everlasting" as the final declaration.

The Creed speaks to the believer to reinforce the ground of faith, bound up in the triune God. The tenets of the gospel are reinforced and put forward to nourish and strengthen faith. It catechizes, capturing biblical teaching with each declaration. By its study, believers are built up in the faith.

The Creed addresses those who have yet to come to faith in Christ by laying before them the God of salvation and the hope of the gospel. It says, "This is what is to be believed." It beckons to Christ as the only way God has given for salvation. It presses the question of whether a person is willing to adopt *the* faith expressed in the Creed as *my* faith. It brings to the table what we must believe and presses the issue of whether we stand on that firm foundation or on sinking sand.

A worship service typically gathers together believers and unbelievers on any given Sunday. The Creed draws a line in the sand in that gathering, distinguishing between those who make its declarations from their hearts and those who make them merely with their mouths. At the same time, it exerts a gravitational pull of truth, beckoning to belief and inviting to embrace Jesus Christ in the gospel. It draws those gathered to be true worshipers, in Spirit and truth.

So the Creed is liturgical (to profess in community), catechetical (to teach), confessional (to express alignment), and missional (as a light to life in Christ). The purpose of this small book is to familiarize the reader with the Christian faith as it unfolds in the profound simplicity of the Apostles' Creed. May the Spirit of the living God enlighten your mind, enflame your heart, and engage your will as you survey the wonders of so great a salvation.

A STAND OF FAITH

I believe.

"I believe." Two simple words that can be life shaping, direction changing, and risk taking. Belief expresses faith, and faith rests on something. Francis Schaeffer famously pointed out that biblical faith is not faith in faith.[1] When we say "I believe," we highlight not merely our faith but the object of our faith. What do we believe in? What merits our confidence? What is worthy of our trust? The object of our faith becomes open to examination.

When our queue in the amusement park finally makes it to the platform for the ride and we take that step into the roller coaster, we believe that we will arrive back exhilarated and safe. Unless we have a death wish, we would not climb aboard if we believed for a second that the ride was dangerous to the point of death. We trust the engineers who designed the ride, the workers who maintain it, and the sixteen-year-old

---

1. Francis Schaeffer, *The God Who Is There* (Downers Grove, Ill.: InterVarsity, 1968), 85.

who operates it. In other words, our faith is not in wishful thinking. Rather, it is grounded in believed reality.

The writer of Hebrews defines faith as "the substance of things hoped for, the evidence of things not seen" (11:1). Many people think of faith as the opposite of fact. "Do you have reason to believe as you do, or is it just a matter of faith?" they will ask. Faith is reduced to personal opinion. It can cater to personal realities—what a person wants to believe, what is true for him or for her. Such faith is not subject to scrutiny, nor would scrutiny be proper. To say "I believe" ends the matter.

But notice the definition just mentioned in the book of Hebrews. Faith is the *substance* of things hoped for. What comes to mind when we think of something substantial? Perhaps a piece of furniture with bulk, made of solid wood— not anything rickety and ready to fall apart if the cat were to jump on it. Substance stands in contrast to the ephemeral, the fleeting.

Such faith comes with certainty and assurance. It is trustworthy. Biblical faith holds the substance of things *hoped for*. Faith is impregnated with hope. *Hope* is another of those words that can be kind of squishy:

Do you think it will rain for the picnic tomorrow?
I don't know, but I *hope* not.

Do you think the team will make the playoffs this year?
I sure *hope* so.

In popular expression, *hope* is more "hope so" than "know so." Biblical hope, however, bears no resemblance to the world's wimpy namesake. Biblical hope offers a confident expectation, an assured conviction, a vibrant certainty that rests on the God of promise and the accomplished work of Jesus Christ. Steel girders of biblical truth make up its foundation. There is nothing iffy about it. The hope proceeds from the substance. We are confident the chair will support our weight, that the roller coaster will make it back to the station, that our salvation is secure.

In 1 Thessalonians, the apostle Paul emphasizes hope. Unlike 1 Corinthians 13:13, where love is given "greatest" billing, in Thessalonians hope receives the accent among the trilogy of Christian virtues: "We give thanks to God always for you all, making mention of you in our prayers, remembering without ceasing your work of faith, labor of love, and patience of hope in our Lord Jesus Christ in the sight of our God and Father, knowing, beloved brethren, your election by God" (1 Thess. 1:2–4; cf. 5:8).

In the body of the letter, the apostle distinguishes between those possessing a hope and those not. The former he calls "brothers." The latter are the "others who have no hope" (4:13). All humanity is divided into two categories: brothers and others, those who have a hope and those who do not. Such is the certainty of this hope Paul extends to the church at Thessalonica that it serves as a solid basis for their comfort and encouragement, a firm foundation to rest on. Notice the "therefore" that drives home the truth presented:

Therefore comfort one another with these words. (4:18)

Therefore comfort each other and edify one another, just as you also are doing. (5:11)

An iffy hope would not be much of a source of comfort.

What is the ground for such assurance for the Christian? What makes the hope of biblical faith "know so" rather than "hope so"? What about hopeful faith fosters comfort and encouragement? The answer is larger than one verse. In fact, the answer derives from the whole of Scripture. But we find a summary statement in 1 Thessalonians in context: "For God did not appoint us to wrath, but to obtain salvation through our Lord Jesus Christ" (5:9). There it is. The ground of hope is the God of grace through the gain of Christ. Christ is the substance of and the foundation for faith. He is the reason for confidence. Solid ground.

The second phrase of the definition of faith in Hebrews 11 states that it is "the evidence of things not seen." When it comes to faith, we don't typically think in terms of evidence. Rather, faith is what kicks in with lack of evidence. When we rest in something that cannot be measured, we say that we just take it on faith. In our empirical age, we tend to scoff at conclusions that cannot be observed, quantified, tested, and verified. We want to hear the evidence, not take things on faith. But biblical faith *does* operate on evidence—the evidence of things *not seen*. We deal in unseen realities on a daily basis.

Right now the room you are in is filled with shows, songs, and information. To perceive and retrieve it, all you have to do is turn on a radio or tap in to the Wi-Fi. That's how faith believes and receives. It appropriates the unseen. Not seen does not mean not real. On the contrary, the things are very much real and are grasped through the spiritual receptors necessary to know them. It is this "know so" that grounds and compels the hope of faith.

The writer of Hebrews lays out this definition of faith as "the substance of things hoped for, the evidence of things not seen" to explain why the saints of old acted as they did. A survey of Hebrews 11 shows people like Abel, Abraham, and Moses functioning by faith. They were not fanciful optimists. They were responsible realists. They believed and acted by faith in the God who had spoken. Here are two examples given in that survey:

> By faith Abraham, when he was tested, offered up Isaac, and he who had received the promises offered up his only begotten son, of whom it was said, "In Isaac your seed shall be called," concluding that God was able to raise him up, even from the dead, from which he also received him in a figurative sense....
>
> By faith Moses, when he became of age, refused to be called the son of Pharaoh's daughter, choosing rather to suffer affliction with the people of God than to enjoy the passing pleasures of sin, esteeming the reproach of Christ greater riches than the treasures in Egypt; for he looked to the reward. (Heb. 11:17–19, 24–26)

The ultimate focus of our faith is the founder of the faith and the foundation of that faith, Jesus Christ. The writer leads us along with the Old Testament saints to Christ: "Therefore we also, since we are surrounded by so great a cloud of witnesses, let us lay aside every weight, and the sin which so easily ensnares us, and let us run with endurance the race that is set before us, looking unto Jesus, the author and finisher of our faith, who for the joy that was set before Him endured the cross, despising the shame, and has sat down at the right hand of the throne of God" (Heb. 12:1–2; see also 11:39–40).

The saints of old set their gaze on the distant horizon of the history that we see clearly in the coming of Christ.

The day was pleasant, so my wife and I took a stroll to an area park that featured a playground with a swing set and some equipment to climb on. A chain-link fence separated the playground from the railroad track that abutted it. The only other person on the playground that day was a little girl, maybe six or seven years old, daintily swaying on one of the swings. The little boy in me could not resist the lure of the swing set and the challenge of seeing how high I could soar.

I took my seat in the swing beside the youngster. Higher and higher I went. The wind rushed by me. On one back-swing, now almost level with the top bar of the swing set, the rubber seat I was sitting on snapped. I went flying backward toward the chain-link fence, like a superhero in rewind, soaring through the air until I came crashing down on my stomach. I was shaken but otherwise unharmed. Shock spread across the little girl's face as she quickly slowed her already unambitious swinging almost to a standstill.

Here's the issue: I had faith the rubber seat of that swing would not only hold me but would also withstand my testing of it as I pushed its limits. I was willing to take a risk because of the strength of my faith. But my faith was only as valid as that rubber seat was strong. Faith perceives realities and rests upon them.

All this gives us an idea of the importance and signifi-cance of uttering the words, "I believe." Through faith we take a stand. As we will see, in embracing the declarations of the Apostles' Creed, we not only relate the Bible's claims but rest in them by faith. In so doing, we insist that claims contrary to the Bible are not only wrong and inadequate but they are contrary to what God has revealed and so in opposition to God Himself. The Creed draws a line in the sand. We see the Bible constantly distinguishing between two options (God versus idols, Baal versus Yahweh, truth versus error, Christ as the only way). In essence, we decide whether to believe God and receive Christ, to whom He testifies, or not. Do we believe Jesus when He says, "I am the way, the truth, and the life. No one comes to the Father except through Me" (John 14:6)? We cannot straddle the fence. We're either in or out, fully invested or not at all, brothers or others.

Since the object of faith stands open to examination, testing, and validation, what does stand as the object of faith for the declarations of the Apostles' Creed? What substance do we rest upon? What evidence do we rely on as the foundation for faith? It all boils down to the revealed truth of the Bible. The Bible makes assertions about God. It lays before us the claims of Christ. A study of the Creed takes us to a study of the Bible as God speaks to the various dimensions and declarations made. It is not that the statements of the Creed are exhaustive, saying everything the Bible teaches, but they are essential. They boil down the Christian faith to those things that are indispensable to believe. The Creed's beauty is not only in its authenticity but also in its simplicity, basic truths that cut across denominational lines and ecclesiastical distinctions. It deals in truth.

What Is Truth?

After He was betrayed by Judas Iscariot and subsequently arrested, Jesus stood before Pontius Pilate, the Roman governor. Pilate tried to ascertain what crime Jesus had committed. Their exchange gets to the heart of the matter.

Jesus answered, "My kingdom is not of this world. If My kingdom were of this world, My servants would fight, so that I should not be delivered to the Jews; but now My kingdom is not from here."

Pilate therefore said to Him, "Are You a king then?"

Jesus answered, "You say rightly that I am a king. For this cause I was born, and for this cause I have come into the world, that I should bear witness to the truth. Everyone who is of the truth hears My voice." (John 18:36–37)

To Jesus's statement Pilate replied, "What is truth?" (v. 38).

What is truth? That's not an easy question to answer. What would you say if a child asked you that? It's one of those deep metaphysical inquiries that defies simple explanation. In fact, John records no answer from Jesus. Perhaps the reason is that the *entire* gospel of John addresses that question.

In his gospel account, John is concerned to distinguish truth from error and to highlight the uniqueness and exclusivity of Jesus as the truth. One of John's favorite words is *witness*. We might think of a witness in a trial who testifies to what he or she has seen. That testimony serves to confirm, to authenticate, to verify. John regularly brings witnesses to the dock to give testimony about Jesus's identity and mission.

He begins his gospel account with John the Baptist: "There was a man sent from God, whose name was John. This man came for a witness, to bear witness of the Light, that all through him might believe. He was not that Light, but was sent to bear witness of that Light" (John 1:6–8). While the other three Gospels call this forerunner John "the Baptist" (e.g., Matt. 3:1; Mark 6:14; Luke 7:20), John the gospel writer never does. For him, he is John the Witness. As a witness he points to Jesus as the Christ who was to come, the Lamb provided by God for the salvation of the world.

Certainly John the Witness *personally* testifies of Jesus, as is recorded in the first chapter of John's gospel:

> Now this is the testimony of John, when the Jews sent priests and Levites from Jerusalem to ask him, "Who are you?"
>
> He confessed, and did not deny, but confessed, "I am not the Christ…
>
> And I have seen and testified that this is the Son of God" (1:19–20, 34).

But it is John the Witness's place in the prologue to John's gospel (1:1–18) that cements his role as witness. Those first eighteen verses provide themes for the rest of the gospel. They open with a new creation account, using the familiar words "in the beginning." Those words bring to mind the first creation account: "In the beginning God created the heavens and the earth" (Gen. 1:1). John's gospel creation account echoes the book of Genesis, with its themes of light and darkness and giving life. The difference is that with the coming of Christ a *new* creation dawns, one redeemed from the effects of the fall that brought the scourge of sin to pervade what God had made good.

We might wonder why John the Witness would find such a prominent place in the few verses of the prologue to John's gospel. It's because of his function as a witness. John stands as a representative of Old Testament prophecy and promise that point to Jesus Christ as the one in whom all is fulfilled. John is the greatest of the Old Testament prophets (cf. Matt. 11:11) because he is the last of its prophets. The One prophesied about has come. The One who *is* Himself the message prophesied has come. He is the Word incarnate (John 1:1, 14).

John the gospel writer fills his book with words of testimony so that the reader is left without a shadow of doubt that Jesus is the Christ who was to come, the Savior of the world. That verdict affects the whole world, both geographically and historically, across generations past, present, and future. Toward the close of his account, John explains the significance of the evidence and verdict that have been put forward: "These are written that you may believe that Jesus is the Christ, the Son of God, and that believing you may have life in His name" (20:31). The weight of evidence has to do with life itself—new life, eternal life.

In recording Pilate's question of what truth is, John puts it to every reader as to what he or she will do about Jesus. Either we are for Him or against Him. We either have life through faith in Him, or we remain in the darkness of sin and unbelief, with the sentence of condemnation hanging over our heads. John puts it in stark terms: "He who believes in Him is not condemned; but he who does not believe is condemned already, because he has not believed in the name of the only begotten Son of God" (3:18). "He who believes in the Son has everlasting life; and he who does not believe the Son shall not see life, but the wrath of God abides on him" (3:36).

So when we come to the Apostles' Creed, we come not to a buffet of beliefs, catering to different tastes for truth. We come to one faith, one ground, one substance, one hope, one redemptive reality. In embracing its declarations, we affirm biblical truth and assert personal faith: that we believe Jesus is the Christ, the Son of God, and that believing we have life in His name. In taking our stand on that truth, we embrace the testimony of Jesus, who declares, "I am the way, the truth, and the life. No one comes to the Father except through Me" (John 14:6).

The evidence amassed by John points us to Christ— eternal, incarnate, blameless, crucified, and risen. To hold to Christ as the truth is not to hold an opinion but to hold the option of life or death evidenced by the Father, as Jesus makes clear: "Most assuredly, I say to you, he who hears My word and believes in Him who sent Me has everlasting life, and shall not come into judgment, but has passed from death into life" (John 5:24).

Believing the Creed

As I write this, spring training has begun for professional baseball. Rookies are learning the ropes and benefiting from the expertise of coaches and trainers. But seasoned players are also learning, or perhaps better put, relearning. Through others' feedback, pitchers are realizing they are dropping their shoulders when they shouldn't. Batters are discovering they have moved too far forward in the batter's box. Adjustments are made.

We can do the same in our Christian faith. There's a point when we need to be indoctrinated so we know what to believe, but there are also times when we need to be reminded of what we believe. A major dimension of the Lord's Supper has to do with remembering. We are to remember the Lord's death until He comes. Why remember? It's because we forget so easily. We take our eyes off Jesus. We lose sight of the gospel, thinking ourselves better than others, more deserving of God's grace, less in need of a Savior. But the sacrament points us to Christ, to Christ alone, to Christ always.

The Creed serves the same function. Like training camp, it brings us back to basics. We can see this in several ways for the well-being of Christ's church.

A Summary of Faith

My furnace bit the dust. I had no complaints. It had lasted over forty years; it had been installed well before I had moved into the house. But cracks had developed in the heat exchanger, allowing for the possible emission of dangerous carbon monoxide. The technician stated the obvious. It had to be replaced. That set me on a course of exploring HVAC companies and furnace models. All the information had my mind awhirl. The options were many, the costs ranging, and the comparisons daunting. But when all the variables were removed, there remained those basic functions that make a furnace a furnace.

What are those basics that make Christianity Christianity? For those seeking to understand the Christian faith, what are the nonnegotiable, irreducible, substantive basics? The Apostles' Creed provides that primer—not that it addresses or even mentions all there is to Christianity, but it does lay out the fundamentals of God, the gospel, and glory.

As I read product brochures and met with sales reps to get my bearings for purchasing a new furnace, so God meets us in the Creed, bringing to bear those essentials for explanation of the Christian faith. The Creed is beautiful in profundity and simplicity. Each statement opens the door to a course of study. Like the furnace literature, the Creed introduces language, themes, and connections that orient the reader to the faith handed down through generations and is relevant for each person—not just for comfort in winter but for comfort in life and in death, as the first question of the Heidelberg Catechism puts it in Trinitarian fashion, as does the Creed:

Q: What is your only comfort in life and in death?

A: That I am not my own, but belong body and soul, in life and in death, to my faithful Savior Jesus Christ. He has fully paid for all my sins with His precious blood, and has set me free from the tyranny of the devil. He also watches over me in such a way that not a hair can fall from my head without the will of my heavenly Father; in fact, all things must work together for my salvation. Because I belong to Him, Christ, by His Holy Spirit, assures me of eternal life, and makes me whole-heartedly willing and ready, from now on to live for Him.

A Statement of Faith

Have you ever seen the outline of a fish on a piece of jewelry or on the bumper sticker of a car? You might be aware of the fish's relationship to Christianity, perhaps saying something about Jesus feeding the five thousand or about Christian mission in being fishers of men. That symbol is called an *ichthus*. *Ichthus* is the Greek word for fish. We find it in the study of fish, ichthyology. The meaning, though, is found in the letters that form the Greek word.

$$I = Iμσούς \text{ (Jesus)}$$
$$X = Χριστος \text{ (Christ)}$$
$$Θ = Θεος \text{ (God)}$$
$$Υ = Υιός \text{ (Son of)}$$
$$Σ = Σωτήρ \text{ (Savior)}$$

The Greek letters that make up the word *ichthus* serve as an acrostic to spell out a statement of faith: Jesus Christ, Son of God, Savior. During Roman times, wearing a fish symbol served as an expression of faith for the early church and a coded testimony to others that you were a believer.

While the Apostles' Creed is not cryptic like the *ichthus*, it too makes a statement of faith, both expressing the Christian faith and making testimony to others. When we say "I believe" and then go on to say what we believe, we make an affirmation and proclaim a pledge of allegiance. We acknowledge the truth it contains and align ourselves with the Author of that truth. J. I. Packer puts our response to God's revelation this way: "I am professing my conviction that God has invited me to this commitment and declaring that I have accepted His invitation."[2]

An Expression of Faith

Reciting the Apostles' Creed is not merely declaring what we acknowledge to be fact. Rather, it is expressing personal faith in the truths contained. We not only recite the historic truths of the Christian faith, we reside in them. We exercise personal faith in the faith of our fathers. This is where the Apostles' Creed becomes the Christian's Creed, where apostolic doctrine is appropriated for personal belief.

By God's grace, He has made us alive in Christ. The statements of the Creed become rich to our taste and nourishing to our soul, savory to the taste buds of spiritual life bestowed by the Holy Spirit. God is glorified through His handiwork of grace. Our expression of faith is evidence of God's saving work in our hearts. John reveals to us the source of saving faith: "But as many as received Him, to them He gave the right to become children of God, to those who believe in

---

2. J. I. Packer, *Affirming the Apostles' Creed* (Wheaton, Ill.: Crossway, 2008), 26.

His name: who were born, not of blood, nor of the will of the flesh, nor of the will of man, but of God" (John 1:12–13; cf. Eph. 2:8–9). The language of the Creed is learned by the conviction of the Spirit and reflects the pedigree of heaven.

Of course, the challenge against empty phrases and vain repetition remains. We don't want to merely rattle off words. Jesus cautions us: "This people honors Me with their lips, but their heart is far from Me" (Mark 7:6). Familiarity can prompt mindlessness. It is easy for us to sing songs, recite prayers, and go through the motions of worship when our heart is not in it. I enjoy coffee in the morning, particularly from my favorite coffee shop. The taste, the aroma, even the whole feel of drinking it while beginning my workday is a delight. There are times, however, when I get so engrossed in the tasks at hand that I realize I finished the whole twenty-ounce cup without having tasted it, let alone savored it. Worship can be like that. Faith must keep its focus. The Creed that should lift our gaze to glory and enflame our hearts is rendered lifeless through the neglect of faith's exercise. Rather than the words becoming means to the end of glorifying God, they become ends in themselves.

The Creed finds itself in the corporate worship of Christ's church, yet it does not lose its individual character. The intensity of "I believe" joins in chorus with others who make the same declaration. We say, "I believe with you. We believe together." We have fellowship in the same Spirit. We give glory to the same Creator God, whom we claim as our mutual Father. We rest in the same Lord Jesus Christ for salvation. We share in the same blessings, all of which are ours through faith in Christ. The Christian's Creed becomes the

Christians' Creed, a symphony of salvation lifted in corporate worship to the glory of our triune God.

To profess is to express personal faith. "I believe." We have faith in *the* faith, the "good thing" (2 Tim. 1:14), that body of truth given by God in the gospel. By grace we establish ourselves not as mere professors of faith but as possessors who are not only sincere but certain by the conviction of the Holy Spirit. In corporate worship that personal faith joins in a chorus of faith unfolded in the declarations of the Creed, to the glory of God.

A Refresher of Faith

Just as the Lord's Supper reminds, reinforces, and refocuses us in the faith, so does the Apostles' Creed. Whether newborn believer or seasoned saint, we all need to hear the gospel regularly. Like a sign whose lettering fades needs periodic touching up, so our awareness of the message of salvation requires regular reminders. The Creed serves as God's touch-up kit to give the truths of God's great work their boldness and luster in our sight.

All of us take things for granted, from our spouses to our daily conveniences. Only when we consciously consider them, only when we delight in what they bring us, only when we give thanks for them will they become more than part of the scenery of our lives.

My favorite stanza in the classic hymn "How Great Thou Art" calls for focused thought:

> And when I think that God his Son not sparing,
> Sent him to die, I scarce can take it in,

That on the cross, my burden gladly bearing,
He bled and died to take away my sin.[3]

As we ponder these things in our hearts, our souls are stirred to sing. God's amazing grace is dusted off from neglect and restored to its place of prominence from the pile of religious relics under which it becomes buried.

Animated by faith, our reciting the Apostles' Creed both gives a refresher course in the gospel and refreshes us in its embrace. While it catechizes the one trying to understand Christianity, it cauterizes the declarations of truth to the seasoned saint.

The Weight of Faith

"I believe," two simple words that hold profound implications, are not unlike "I do" in a marriage ceremony. They are weighty words, expressing commitment and relationship with the God who has invited us to Himself. They carry both privilege and responsibility. They declare deliverance from the dominion of darkness and allegiance to the kingdom of life and light in Jesus Christ for life, liberty, and the pursuit of holiness.

Creed relates to belief. A creed is a statement of faith, an expression of what we believe. It is one way we make our invisible faith visible. *The Invisible Man* was a 1933 science fiction movie starring Claude Rains in the title role. Rains played a scientist who developed a way to become invisible. He could be seen only when wearing clothes, or in Rain's case, bandages. In like fashion, the beliefs of our invisible

---

3. Stuart K. Hine, "How Great Thou Art," in *Trinity Hymnal*, rev. ed. (Suwanee, Ga.: Great Commission Publications, 1990), #44.

faith take shape when we clothe them with the statements of the Creed. We display our faith and we allow public scrutiny.

On a trip to London, my wife and I worshiped with an evangelical congregation on a Sunday. The church was fairly new, but it met in an old building. The worship environment was beautiful, rich in history and appealing to the eye. On the wall at the front of the sanctuary I noticed an ornate plaque of the Apostles' Creed. In large letters calligraphed at the top were the words "I believe." Under that came the Creed itself in regular type, about a quarter of the size of the stylized opening line.

Several things struck me as I saw that plaque. One was the visible presence of the invisible faith in England as it was in the United States, and so would be around the world. Another was that this statement of faith had been there for years, binding generations together to a single faith, an exhibit of the gospel of Jesus Christ. But what particularly occurred to me was the conspicuousness of those opening words, "I believe." They dwarfed the actual Creed itself. They were not part of the substance of the Creed, but they held prominence in respect to the declarations that followed. It reminded me of a dynamite blasting cap. The explosive is present, real, and cataclysmic. But without the blasting cap, it is rendered ineffective. Faith is that catalyst to the content of the Creed for the one reciting it.

Belief is not part of the Creed, but it is what, by God's grace, activates it for personal salvation. Belief brings the weight of truth to weigh on our hearts, embracing us like a heavy comforter on a cold, winter day. Now we turn to those declarations that exhibit the faith we hold, beginning with a belief in God.

THE GOD

I believe in God.

The year was about AD 75. The apostle Paul was on his second missionary journey. He had traveled in the Macedonian peninsula from Thessalonica to Berea and had made his way to Athens, Greece. Athens was the center of Greek culture and was associated with the likes of Socrates, Aristotle, and Plato. We can picture the scene. The ancient ruins that we witness today are intact and busy with activity. Men in flowing robes walk the roads engaged in philosophical debate.

As the apostle strolls about the city, he finds himself becoming greatly agitated. His mission is to spread the gospel, declaring the mercies of God in Jesus Christ. Yet all around him stand idols, primarily statues to all sorts of gods. Those familiar with Greek mythology would recognize the names of Zeus, Athena, and Ares. The city is teeming with them.

As was his custom, Paul visited the local synagogue to explain to the Jews and other interested parties that Jesus is the Christ they had been expecting, the One promised and prophesied about throughout the Old Testament. He reasoned with them from the Scriptures why it was necessary for Jesus as the Messiah to suffer and to rise from the dead.

Among the interested parties were some philosophers. Evidently they had a religious bent, judging by what piqued their interest in Paul's teaching, as Luke records: "'He seems to be a proclaimer of foreign gods,' because he preached to them Jesus and the resurrection." They called him a "babbler," but still they wanted to hear in greater detail what Paul had to say (Acts 17:18). It wasn't that they were necessarily inclined to be swayed by Paul's teaching, but they were like "breaking news junkies," and Paul offered something new to the ear that intrigued them. In his account on Paul's time in Athens, Luke writes, "All the Athenians and the foreigners who were there spent their time in nothing else but either to tell or to hear some new thing" (Acts 17:21). Paul was proclaiming good news, and the ears of these thinkers were tuned in.

Paul complied with their desire to hear more and stood in the middle of the Areopagus to address the gathered group of philosophers. Here's how he began: "Men of Athens, I perceive that in all things you are very religious; for as I was passing through and considering the objects of your worship, I even found an altar with this inscription: TO THE UNKNOWN GOD" (Acts 17:22–23).

The apostle knew his audience, at least to a degree. He didn't reach in his satchel and bring out some well-used sermon or oft-repeated lecture to give to them. No, he had just walked around the city and observed its idolatry. He surmised from his observations that they were religious—very religious judging by the abundance of idols and altars. We might say they were quite spiritual, holding to something greater than themselves. But more than that, they were worshipers. They gave these gods veneration and accolades in keeping with the particular deity's area of focus. Like physicians in our day, these gods had specializations and so were to be sought for harvest, for war, for love, even for various terrains like land, air, or sea.

Paul met them where they were. In his meanderings around Athens, he had noticed another altar. This one was not to any particular god but to an unknown god. That makes sense. If your success at the harvest or in war depended on your appeasing the appropriate deity by sacrificing food stuff or the like to him or her, it would be disastrous to overlook a god. An altar to an unknown god would be a miscellaneous category, a catchall to cover the deific bases. Paul used this as a launching point for preaching. "Therefore, the One whom you worship without knowing, Him I proclaim to you" (Acts 17:23).

Before we get into what Paul proclaimed we need to ask, Just who does Paul think he is that he has the audacity to tell them they don't know what they are doing, but he does? Who is to say that Paul's God is any better than the Greek gods? Isn't that an affront to other cultures, a cultural imperialism of sorts?

Those are questions that relate to *how* we know about God. By what authority do we believe what we believe? Paul's authority was the Bible. Earlier in Acts 17, at Thessalonica he taught and explained and reasoned *from the Scriptures* (vv. 2–3). At his next stop in Berea, before heading to Athens, his teaching was authenticated from the Scriptures: "They received the word with all readiness, and searched the Scriptures daily to find out whether these things were so" (v. 11). Paul's sole source of authority was the Word of God, what God Himself had revealed through His servants the prophets and caused to be written down (inscripturated) for study and examination. What Paul would make known to the philosophers in Athens was not, "This is what I think," or "This is one possibility." Rather, Paul would declare, "This is what God says about Himself in the Bible." As Paul would put it elsewhere: "For I received from the Lord that which I also delivered to you" (1 Cor. 11:23).

Paul begins his message to the Greek philosophers with a shocker: "God, who made the world and everything in it, since He is Lord of heaven and earth, does not dwell in temples made with hands. Nor is He worshiped with men's hands, as though He needed anything, since He gives to all life, breath, and all things" (Acts 17:24–25). Right out of the gate Paul drops a bombshell when he speaks of "God"—not gods, but God. Remember, Athens in that day was polytheistic. They believed in a multitude of deities. They recognized a whole pantheon of gods. To speak of one God would have been cold water to the face, causing them to lean forward in their seats.

Paul goes on to challenge their whole theology. This one God is not only the Creator of everything but He is Lord over all that He has made. He is not a regional God. He is not a specialty God. He is not a chief God. He is *the* God, the only God. Contrary to their idols, He is the true and living God.

In fact, one of the telltale signs of saving faith for us is recognizing God as true and living in contrast to false and lifeless idols. Paul attests to that when he writes to the church at Thessalonica, the city he had visited earlier in Acts 17 before arriving at Athens:

> For from you the word of the Lord has sounded forth, not only in Macedonia and Achaia, but also in every place. Your faith toward God has gone out, so that

we do not need to say anything. For they themselves declare concerning us what manner of entry we had to you, and how you turned to God from idols to serve the living and true God, and to wait for His Son from heaven, whom He raised from the dead, even Jesus who delivers us from the wrath to come. (1 Thess. 1:8–10)

"Living and true" is basically code for *real* as opposed to idols that are false gods. It begs the question of what we embrace as truth and where we place our faith and our hope.

It gets better. Paul declares not only that there is but one God, the uncreated Creator who rules over every inch of what He has made, but also that He is not in need of anyone. The self-existent God is self-sufficient. For the Athenians each god had an address, a place where the grocer could deliver the foodstuff as offerings. But the real God doesn't live in a temple made by humans. As Solomon, a great king of the Old Testament, pointed out in the dedication of the temple of ancient Israel: "But will God indeed dwell with men on the earth? Behold, heaven and the heaven of heavens cannot contain You. How much less this temple which I have built!" (2 Chron. 6:18). The temple attested to God's presence among His people, but it did not house God.

The ancient Greeks had things turned around. The gods they understood were needy and in some sense dependent. But the living and true God was never needy, never dependent. On the contrary, they needed Him—in every way, all the time. He is the one from whom life itself comes—every breath breathed and everything else. He is the giver, the sustainer. He is a good God who showers His creatures with good things to enjoy. This God is of a wholly different ilk from the gods they supposed.

The gods they imagined had office hours when they could be approached according to various needs, like visiting the doctor or a congressional representative to address a problem and get action on it. But the real God was sovereign, and His providence ruled over all He had made: "And He has made from one blood every nation of men to dwell on all the face of the earth, and has determined their preappointed times and the boundaries of their dwellings" (Acts 17:26). This God made, designed, determined, appointed—all those things that showed Him to be vastly different from their idols and from those who manufactured them (see Ps. 115:8).

Here is where Paul starts to get personal. He moves from theology proper, the study of God, to applied theology. What does this mean for me? What does this say about how I can recognize and respond appropriately to the true God? After explaining that God is greater than they could possibly fathom and is not distant but involved, Paul presses on:

> So that they should seek the Lord, in the hope that they might grope for Him and find Him, though He is not far from each one of us; for in Him we live and move and have our being, as also some of your own poets have said, 'For we are also His offspring.' Therefore, since we are the offspring of God, we ought not to think that the Divine Nature is like gold or silver or stone, something shaped by art and man's devising." (Acts 17:27–29)

The apostle highlights the point of connection. How can they know this God? How can they connect with Him? How can they understand Him properly? The answer begins with see-ing themselves made in the image of the real God.

The polytheists had made gods in their image. They had fashioned a god as they imagined him to be or wanted her to be, a god constructed according to their fancy, meeting their specifications. We see that in present-day conceptions of God. God is depicted as larger than life, with a flowing white beard. Or God is said to be one with nature, or one with us, an impersonal force. Some see Him as a cosmic watchmaker, creating the universe, setting it in motion, and retiring to His study. Others see God as distant and unknown—and in fact unknowable. Every spirituality has its own version of God, crafted by the imaginations of people.

But Paul says that God, the personal God, is our reality. The Greek poets in a sense had it right: in God we do "live and move and have our being" (Acts 17:28). His is an inherent being. Ours is a derived being. God alone has being within Himself. We find a picture of this in God's first encounter with Moses at a bush that burned but was not consumed by the fire. The bush was not fuel for the fire; the flame had being in itself (see Exodus 3). From that display, God revealed His name: I AM (Ex. 3:14). God exists beyond the created, beyond time. He is self-existent. No matter how immense we imagine God to be, our understanding falls short if we conceive Him to be part of creation.

What the Greek philosophers had done in constructing their gods was miss the cardinal point: God is not made in the image of man. We are made in His. Think for a moment about what it means to bear an image. When you look in the mirror and you see your reflection, which holds the reality and the honor—you or your image? You, of course. We hold reality and glory as reflections, but the reflected holds the greater glory, like the moon to the sun. Glory goes not to the image-bearer but to the One whose image is borne. If we serve a god as we imagine him to be, then we make a god in our image and make ourselves the creator who is to be praised. Every human as a created being bears the image of God, even to the extent that they can consider themselves offspring of God (see Acts 17:29).

Moreover, bearing God's image places each of us under His ownership and authority. Jesus was asked by the religious leaders of His day if they should pay taxes or not. Their question was not sincere but came from a desire to get Jesus in trouble with the Roman authorities. Jesus, however, used it as a teaching opportunity:

> But Jesus perceived their wickedness, and said, "Why do you test Me, you hypocrites? Show Me the tax money."
>
> So they brought Him a denarius.
>
> And He said to them, "Whose image and inscription is this?"
>
> They said to Him, "Caesar's."
>
> And He said to them, "Render therefore to Caesar the things that are Caesar's, and to God the things that are God's." (Matt. 22:18–21)

Do you see what Jesus did? He wasn't speaking of the separation of church and state; rather, He was showing the importance of bearing an image. The state had a right to collect taxes because the image of Caesar on the coinage reflected the authority of government and the responsibilities of citizenry. Underlying Jesus's message is a more profound, foundational premise. The denarius bore the emperor's image, along with all that meant. Who bears God's image, along with all that means? We humans do. Bearing an image is a mark of ownership and accountability. It invokes rights and responsibilities.

That's why Paul segues to this: "Truly, these times of ignorance God overlooked, but now commands all men everywhere to repent, because He has appointed a day on which He will judge the world in righteousness by the Man whom He has ordained. He has given assurance of this to all by raising Him from the dead" (Acts 17:30–31). The God who created and rules over all makes demands of acknowledgment and allegiance by those fashioned in His image.

We can see that our view of God makes a vast difference in how we see ourselves and how we approach life. The God we believe in affects our understanding of salvation, and affirmation of the biblical God is the starting point for the Apostles' Creed. We want to conform our view of God to how God introduces Himself to us in the Bible. In fact, the tone for any discussion of religion begins with the God believed in and the basis for that belief. Is He a made-up God as we want Him to be, or the Maker God who wants us to embrace Him as He reveals Himself to be? Made up is the same as make believe, so no matter how profound or sincere our belief about God, it is to the true and living God we will give account.

What God?

Paul was on a gospel mission. He was appointed by God to take the message of the Messiah, the good news of salvation in His name, to the nations. Yet here he arrives in Athens, invited by an interested audience, and he doesn't talk about that Messiah until the end of his message, and even then not by name. Instead, he gives vague reference to "the Man whom He has ordained. He has given assurance of this to all by raising Him from the dead" (Acts 17:31). The New King James translation begins the word "Man" with a capital letter, letting readers know that Paul is speaking of Jesus, but Paul's hearers would not have received even that clue in spoken form.

Paul did not begin his evangelistic message by speaking about the Christ, but by speaking about the Creator. God was the starting point. What his listeners believed about God would affect their understanding of life, of themselves, of their need, and the provision for that need. That's why, in the Apostles' Creed, God is the starting point for belief. We need to acknowledge the living God in order to understand ourselves and our need that only He can meet. When Paul brought the gospel message to the people of Athens, he wasn't trying to replace one religious system with another, nor was he saying that his religion was better. Rather, he was proclaiming truth, the truth of a message he had received from God that had supernaturally transformed his own life. The target was not the Greek culture. It was people's hearts. Only the Holy Spirit could produce change at the heart level. Paul admitted elsewhere that his theological precision, debating prowess, or eloquence of speech could not manufacture that change (see 1 Cor. 2:1–5). Only the Spirit could. Paul proclaimed his message with the contentment and confidence that the Spirit would work His work.

Paul's encounter with the philosophers in Athens serves as a good reminder for our gospel interactions with people. We want to listen. Just as Paul listened by surveying the city that observed not just idols but a bevy of idols, so we want to listen for others' understanding of God and the origin of that understanding. The God they embrace will affect their view of the work of Jesus as the Christ of God.

In discussing the idea of an understanding of God, a friend of mine reminded me of the story about the group of blind men trying to determine what an elephant was based on the part of the pachyderm they happened to touch. The one who touched the tail thought an elephant was like a snake; the one who touched the leg thought an elephant was like a tree trunk. My friend's point was that they were all describing the same animal, only from different and limited perspectives. She concluded, "Isn't that exactly what man does when he tries to define God? God is all the things people think and more. So are people 'designing' God, or are they simply 'defining' God based on what they 'touch'?"

My friend's point demonstrates the importance of informed faith that was the subject of my first chapter. Otherwise, our ideas will be formed on the basis of our experience or preference, and truth will be simply subjective and arbitrary. In our conversations with people about the gospel, we want to listen to where they got their ideas about God. Do they understand God from a tragic life experience, from a snippet cherry-picked from the Bible, or even from a religious system contrary to the Bible?

Over the years, I have encountered all sorts of notions about God, ranging from the extraordinarily fanciful to the scrupulously selective. For example, people will often differentiate between the God of the Old Testament and the God of the New Testament, as though they were different deities. The God of the Old Testament is thought to be wrathful, cruel, and vindictive while the God of the New Testament is loving, kind, and beneficent.

Some who fashion a designer god will pick characteristics like they would choose from paint samples. "My god is a god of love. He would never send anyone to hell. And he's certainly not a wrathful god." "God allowed my son to be killed in a car accident. I believe God is good, so He must not have been attentive or able to prevent it." People pick and choose what they like. If you do present biblical evidence to the contrary, they may respond, "Well, that's not the kind of God I believe in." In so doing, they commit the sin of the Athenians, forming a god by their own art and imaginings (see Acts 17:29). Ironically, they become the creator instead of acknowledging themselves as the creatures and giving glory to the actual Creator who is to be forever praised.

God and the Gospel

Our conception of God makes all the difference for our understanding of the gospel.[1] If we hold that God is simply a God of love to the neglect of His holiness, then His justice and wrath seem to make Him schizophrenic, a Jekyll and Hyde. Only a proper understanding of God will fully embrace the right and even the necessity of God's requirement that Paul brings home to the Athenian pundits: "Truly, these times of ignorance God overlooked, but now commands all men everywhere to repent, because He has appointed a day on which He will judge the world in righteousness" (Acts 17:30–31). A permissive, doting, benign god would not make demands for repentance and certainly would not be in the business of judging.

Yet the God who reveals Himself in the Bible is *both* loving and just. In fact, His love is fully grasped in the context

---

1. Read Isaiah 46 to see the absurdity of trusting in designer gods.

of His wrath. Consider two passages, both from the New Testament, both rooted in the Old Testament and realized in the New Testament with the coming of Jesus Christ. The first passage is from John's gospel:

> And as Moses lifted up the serpent in the wilderness, even so must the Son of Man be lifted up, that whoever believes in Him should not perish but have eternal life. For God so loved the world that He gave His only begotten Son, that whoever believes in Him should not perish but have everlasting life. For God did not send His Son into the world to condemn the world, but that the world through Him might be saved.
>
> He who believes in Him is not condemned; but he who does not believe is condemned already, because he has not believed in the name of the only begotten Son of God. (3:14–18)

The incident from the Old Testament book of Numbers (21:1–9) describes God providing the remedy for the people's rebellion. God was judging the people for their rebellion by sending poisonous snakes to bite them. They were dying right and left. God instructed Moses to affix a bronze serpent to a pole and lift it up for the people to look to. All who looked to God's provision, believing it to heal, would be spared from death.

The serpent mounted to the pole serves as a type and preview for God's giving His Son, who was lifted up on the cross, that whoever believes on Him will not perish spiritually but have eternal life. The giving of the snake speaks to God's mercy and grace. The people with Moses deserved to die, but God did not treat them as their sins deserved. Rather, He graciously provided an antidote—actually *the* antidote—to be received by faith, believing God and trusting in His provision. In like fashion, God sent His Son into the world to bear the sin of His people on the cross so that those who deserved to die would not perish in their sin and rebellion. All who look to Him in faith will be saved.

Why did God send His Son? What compelled Him to do such an amazing thing? The answer John records for us is love. God so loved the world. In His unexpected, undeserved, unearned grace, God gave His Son over to death. In so doing, God remained true to His holy character as righteous and just while at the same time exhibiting His mercy, grace, and love. But love is often misunderstood, repackaged with toothless sentimentalism so that even when people say that God is a God of love and not wrath, the love becomes powerless.

God is not loving *or* just. He reveals Himself as both. Like a burst of light in a pitch-black night sky, He displays the light of His love against the bleak, black backdrop of His wrath. If the word "perish" is removed from John 3:16, the love of God makes no sense. Try it. Recite John 3:16 and leave out the "should not perish" part. The point and the potency of what God has done are lost. Just like the mercy of God is set against the context of death with the poisonous snakes, the love of God shines gloriously against the ominous backdrop of perishing in condemnation for sin's guilt. It is against that foreboding context that love is displayed with such astounding beauty. Without that background of condemnation, the love God shows loses its marvel. In other words, the love of God is not seen despite the cross but in the cross. The cross of Christ is where the love of God erupts in glorious display, where God's wrath and mercy meet. If we design our own god, we demean the cross and defame the God who gave His Son to be our substitute.

The second example of how love and justice coalesce can be seen in Paul's explanation of the gospel in his letter to the Romans. The question posed in the early part of Romans asks how God can be true to His holy character that demands justice while being true to His promises to free the ungodly from the guilt of their sin and the condemnation they deserve. Again, we see the love and just wrath of God not in opposition but in collaboration: "But God demonstrates His own love toward us, in that while we were still sinners, Christ died for us. Much more then, having now been justified by His blood, we shall be saved from wrath through Him" (5:8–9).

God's exercise of love comes to us *as sinners.* God did not pardon our sins; He paid for them. He met our debt and satisfied His wrath through Jesus Christ. His justice is upheld. The guilt of sin is not ignored or swept under the carpet. That guilt is atoned for, and God's justice is preserved. The character of God is honored. We are sobered by the death of Christ.

The God of the Creed

Just as Paul began with a view of God in his message to the polytheistic Greek philosophers, so the starting point for the Apostles' Creed is a consideration of God. We make eye contact in faith with the God we believe in. Lifting our eyes to the living and true God establishes the perspective needed for the purpose of the Creed and the manner in which it unfolds. The work of Christ and the giving of the Spirit flow out of the person and purpose of God. In this sense, the Creed tells a story, a story that begins with the God of the Bible and carries His saving purpose.

Certainly the Apostles' Creed holds up a triune God. The God proclaimed exists in triunity. He is one God, perpetually existing in three persons. Each person of the Godhead—the Father, the Son, and the Holy Spirit—is fully God, eternally in communion with one another. The three sections of the Creed speak to belief in the God of the Bible. That belief distinguishes itself from monotheism, polytheism, deism, and atheism. It attests to the God who is more than a supreme being, more than some sort of life source or impersonal force. He is more than a designer from which the complexities and consistencies of creation are understood. To say we believe in God is not just an affirmation that we are not atheists and that we are theists, believing in a god. Rather, we declare we believe in *the* God, the living and true God, the God of the Bible, in conformity with His self-revelation in the Bible.

But we don't get all that from the Creed itself. In fact, the first declaration about God the Father is extremely brief: "I believe in God the Father almighty, Maker of heaven and earth." That's it. No discussion given to the scope of God's revelation spread across the pages of the Bible. Yet this God in His fullness is the one the Creed holds up for faith. This God is where salvation begins. We know that from the remainder of the declarations. Jesus is introduced to us in respect to this God as "His only Son." The work of Jesus and the blessings of the Spirit relate to the nature of God and His promises of redemption that proceed from Him.

What this says to us is that while the God of the Apostles' Creed is the God of the Bible and therefore exists in three persons, the threefold structure of the Creed is not only intended to teach that God is triune. The Creed does not lay out a theology of God. Rather, it relates a story of the outworking of redemption by God—Father, Son, and Holy Spirit. The Trinity is important to affirm. But the three-part flow of the Creed around the members of the Godhead functions more like a video portrayal of God on the move than a still portrait of God in His eternal being. Unlike the Nicene Creed, which arose out of doctrinal conflict and was settled by a church council to affirm the deity and equality of the Son and the Holy Spirit, the Apostles' Creed expresses a basic reality of the Christian gospel. While upholding the Trinity, it unfurls a salvation that is Trinitarian. It portrays a God at work for us and for our salvation. The story told is the story of the gospel, unfolded in God the Father who appointed our salvation, God the Son incarnate to accomplish our salvation, and God the Spirit of the risen Son to apply salvation and bring Christ to us along with every blessing of salvation wrought by Him. At every point, our eyes are stayed on *the* God.

The Apostles' Creed catechizes in the gospel. Jesus as God's only Son is presented in His person and in His saving work as the basis for faith. His work is understood in respect to the God first mentioned in the Creed. Jesus as the Son of God is not just the Son in eternal relation to the Father but the Son sent by the Father to save. Let's now explore what is said about God—what it means to believe in Him as the Father, Maker of heaven and earth.

3

FATHER AND MAKER

I believe in God, the Father almighty,
Maker of heaven and earth.

Have you ever mingled at a gathering where you were meeting people for the first time? Perhaps it was a formal function, like a wedding reception or business gathering, with people dressed up in finery circulating around the room. How does the conversation usually go? Usually there is greeting and exchanging of names. From there you might ask where they are from, moving on to what sort of work they do, along with their background and credentials. In your conversation you might search for common ground that you can explore together, such as hobbies or travel experiences. In talking about what brings them to that function, you start to form an idea of relationship, perhaps their relationship to the bride or their place in the company hierarchy.

Just as that conversation shapes opinion, so the opening to the Apostles' Creed introduces us to God and how we are to recognize Him. In so doing, we understand ourselves in relationship to Him. He is not only God but He is God the

Father, God the Maker. His credentials are put forth and His relationship to us established.

Right away, though, we might be caught a bit off guard. Why is God spoken of as Father before He is identified as Maker? We would think the logical order would be Creator and then Redeemer, the creation preceding the fall—unless perhaps He is called Father in respect to His eternal relationship with Jesus. Does that mean our introduction to God in the opening words of the Creed is Christ-centered, as God is introduced in respect to the Son, much like a distinguished gentleman we meet at a party might say that he is the father of the bride? His identity is swallowed up in the reason for the event. Also, why is God called "the Father almighty"? We find in the Bible the expression "God almighty" but never "Father almighty." With these sorts of questions in mind, we turn to what we mean when we say that we believe in God as the Father almighty and Maker of heaven and earth.

Relevance and Reverence

In confessing God for who He is, the Creed opens with overtones of worship. This God is the Creator who is to be forever praised. He has sought people to worship Him. He has turned our hearts from idols to acknowledge and adore Him as God. To invoke the name of God is to provoke His praise. Robert Rayburn speaks to this reflex when he describes a gathering for worship: "Corporate Christian worship is the activity of a congregation of true believers in which they seek to render to God that adoration, praise, confession, intercession, thanksgiving, and obedience to which He is entitled by virtue of the ineffable glory of His person and the magnificent grace of His acts of redemption in Jesus Christ."[1] Worship belongs to God for who He is and what He has done and is stirred by faith-fueled acknowledgment of these things.

We find this dual emphasis recognizing God as Maker and Redeemer in our hymnody. Our hearts swell with praise to our Savior God in "How Great Thou Art," which reflects on "the awesome wonder" of "all the worlds" His "hands have made" and then considers "that God, His Son not sparing, sent Him to die." Likewise the Psalter, God's inspired hymnbook, celebrates the glory of God through this dual acknowledgment. Notice, for example, Psalm 136, which opens by affirming that God is Creator and so deserving of praise:

> Oh, give thanks to the LORD, for He is good!
>   For His mercy endures forever.
> Oh, give thanks to the God of gods!
>   For His mercy endures forever.
> Oh, give thanks to the Lord of lords!
>   For His mercy endures forever:
>
> To Him who alone does great wonders,
>   For His mercy endures forever;
> To Him who by wisdom made the heavens,
>   For His mercy endures forever;
> To Him who laid out the earth above the waters,
>   For His mercy endures forever;
> To Him who made great lights,
>   For His mercy endures forever—
> The sun to rule by day,
>   For His mercy endures forever;

---

1. Robert G. Rayburn, *O Come, Let Us Worship* (Grand Rapids: Baker, 1980), 21.

> The moon and stars to rule by night,
>> For His mercy endures forever. (vv. 1–9)

Clearly the psalmist leads us in a chorus of praise to God as Maker of heaven and earth. But then he goes on to say that this Creator God is not only our Maker; He is our Redeemer who intervened in the course of history to save a people for His own possession. The psalmist recounts much more of that history, but a few verses will suffice to make the point. Here he refers to the exodus, when God rescued His people from bondage in Egypt, the Old Testament picture of God's gracious and powerful deliverance:

> To Him who struck Egypt in their firstborn,
>> For His mercy endures forever;
> And brought out Israel from among them,
>> For His mercy endures forever;
> With a strong hand, and with an outstretched arm,
>> For His mercy endures forever;
> To Him who divided the Red Sea in two,
>> For His mercy endures forever....
>
> Who remembered us in our lowly state,
>> For His mercy endures forever;
> And rescued us from our enemies,
>> For His mercy endures forever. (vv. 10–13, 23–24)

Notice the refrain to each of these statements: "For His mercy endures forever." Each description of God, each act of God—the entire narrative is punctuated with praise. More than that, the refrain speaks of God's mercy. The word in the original is difficult to capture with a single English equivalent. It carries the idea of gracious steadfast love and faithful mercies. The word relates to God's intention to save a people for Himself. Our Creator is our Redeemer!

The opening words of the Creed that cite these credentials of God bring us to holy ground on holy business. They have relevance for us who utter them in faith and evoke a reverence of worship and awe of the God we acclaim. They help us behold God in His glory and grace. The tone they set keeps us from reading the rest of the Creed with dry formality or bored monotone. To recite the Creed is to engage with God Himself.

Now we turn to a closer examination of what is meant by the words chosen for introducing God. We begin by exploring what it means for us to declare that God is the Maker of heaven and earth, and then we will return to God as Father almighty.

Maker of Heaven and Earth

The cardinal sin that indicts all of humankind is refusal to acknowledge God as the Creator and to give Him the glory due His name. It is the iniquity of image-bearers who suppose themselves to be autonomous of the One whose image they bear. In this iniquity, sinners make themselves to be god, supposing themselves to be the arbiters of good and evil, living lives of self-determination without regard for their Maker.

In his letter to the church at Rome, Paul makes it clear that the witness of creation testifies to a Creator: "For since the creation of the world His invisible attributes are clearly seen, being understood by the things that are made, even His eternal power and Godhead, so that they are without excuse" (1:20). The heavens declare the glory of God. He is the one who determines the number of stars and calls them each by name. The vastness, the order, the intricacy, and the splendor of what has been made all point to a Creator, like a magnificent sculpture bears witness to an unsurpassed sculptor.

By this witness of what has been made, the apostle invites us to study the canvas of creation to get an inkling of the glory of God. Any with eyes to see will behold a creator and designer and perceive His eternity, creativity, and power. With that, they will perceive themselves to be finite and frail.

But therein is the rub. People need eyes to see. Paul indicts all humankind for not only failing to see but also refusing to see. They deny what creation makes apparent. The apostle puts it in moral terms: they suppress the truth by their unrighteousness (Rom. 1:18). Paul explains: "Although they knew God, they did not glorify Him as God, nor were thankful, but became futile in their thoughts, and their foolish hearts were darkened. Professing to be wise, they became fools, and changed the glory of the incorruptible God into an image made like corruptible man—and birds and four-footed animals and creeping things" (Rom. 1:21–23).

Just as image-bearers came to see themselves independent of the One whose image they bore, they came to the absurdity of worshiping the creation rather than the Creator. Paul puts it in stark terms, saying they "exchanged the truth of God for the lie, and worshiped and served the creature rather than the Creator, who is blessed forever" (Rom. 1:25). God has designed humankind to be worshipers, but worshiping anything or anyone other than the Creator is a worship disorder, like the anomaly of ducklings lined up to follow a cat.

So to recognize God as "Maker of heaven and earth" marks a reversal of the indictment of Romans 1. It attests to the intervention of God to shine light into the darkness of a foolish heart, a darkness of sin and unbelief that has rejected the revelation of God and gone its own way. It testifies to a new creating work by God. The apostle speaks to new creating work at the personal level: "For it is the God who commanded light to shine out of darkness, who has shone in our hearts to give the light of the knowledge of the glory of God in the face of Jesus Christ" (2 Cor. 4:6).

Blind eyes that now see and foolish, darkened hearts now enlightened attest to God's power to deliver from the dominion of darkness that is this fallen world (Eph. 2:1–8; 4:17–22). That some people believe in God as Creator at its heart means God has sought such worshipers and turned Romans 1 on its head by His redeeming power and amazing grace.

But what about believing God to be the Maker of *heaven and earth*? What about Jupiter, Mars, and the other planets? What about the millions of other solar systems that sprawl through the universe? Is the language of the Creed restrictive?

To say that God made heaven and earth is not to limit God or to localize God's work, ascribing only some of creation to Him. Rather, the expression speaks to all that has been made. We can trace "Creator of heaven and earth" throughout Scripture to discover that the phrase applies to the true and living God who is separate from creation as eternal and uncreated. Paul identifies the living God as the Creator God: "the living God, who made the heaven, the earth, the sea, and all things that are in them" (Acts 14:15). This is the God Paul declares to the philosophers at Athens: "God, who made the world and everything in it…is Lord of heaven and earth" (Acts 17:24). The phrase "heaven and earth" is shorthand for *all* that has been made. Maker of heaven and earth is a credential of the uncreated Creator apart from His creation. King Hezekiah captures the unique glory of God in his prayer: "O LORD of hosts, God of Israel, the One who dwells between the cherubim, You are God, You alone, of all the kingdoms of the earth. You have made heaven and earth" (Isa. 37:16). Jesus also referred to His Father in this way: "In that hour Jesus rejoiced in the Spirit and said, 'I thank You, Father, Lord of heaven and earth, that You have hidden these things from the wise and prudent and revealed them to babes. Even so, Father, for so it seemed good in Your sight'" (Luke 10:21).

When the psalmist declares that His help comes from the Lord, who made heaven and earth (Pss. 121:1–2; 124:8), he is saying that his confidence rests on One unbound by the limitations of this world. Paul says much the same thing in laying out the ground of the believer's confidence: "For I am persuaded that neither death nor life, nor angels nor principalities nor powers, nor things present nor things to come, nor height nor depth, nor any other created thing, shall be able to separate us from the love of God which is in Christ Jesus our Lord" (Rom. 8:38–39). All that belongs to the created order is set on one side, and God is set on the other as distinct, unmovable, and certain. It is this God in His glory whom the Creed beckons us to acknowledge and adore.

The Father Almighty

What does it mean to declare that God is the Father almighty? Is He Father in reference to Christians who make the declaration, or in reference to Christ "His only Son," as the second section of the Apostles' Creed begins? Unlike the model prayer that Jesus taught His disciples, the Creed does not say "our Father" but "the Father." And why "almighty"? Usually that would be descriptive of God as Creator, not Father.

Again we are reminded of the purpose of the Creed in not only affirming that God is triune but that He is the eternally existent God at work for the redemption of sinners through His Son. The truths of the Apostles' Creed are embraced by us, believers who have received such a great salvation, beneficiaries of the appointment of the Father, the accomplishment of the Son, and the application of Christ's accomplished work to us by the Spirit. In speaking of God as Father, the Creed begins on a note of relationship and suggests something is afoot, setting the tone for what is to come. God is described as He is for His role as Redeemer. Such a description reminds us of the language of the prophet Isaiah:

> For your Maker is your husband,
> The LORD of hosts is His name;
> And your Redeemer is the Holy One of Israel;
> He is called the God of the whole earth. (Isa. 54:5)

"Father almighty" seems to be an expression of the early church fathers, recognizing the living God in loving relationship.[2] We are not pressed to distinguish between God as the Father of His only begotten Son and God as the adoptive Father of all who have faith in Christ. He is the God and Father of our Lord Jesus Christ. By virtue of Christ's redemption, He is the God and Father of those united to Christ by faith.

---

2. Both Irenaeus (120–202) and Hippolytus of Rome (170–235) use the expression "Father almighty" in their apologetics for the Christian faith in reference to God the Father in the Trinity and in His role in the work of salvation along with the Son and the Holy Spirit.

Writing can be tricky nowadays. When I was in grammar school we were taught that if even a single male was included among a group of females, the masculine pronoun was to be used. For example, "The youth group had a great time at the amusement park. Everyone went on the rides of his own choice." The reason this makes writing tricky today is that it's no longer considered acceptable to use the masculine pronoun in reference to a group that includes both genders, but it's awkward to keep saying "his or her" all the time. In fact, it's becoming acceptable to say "their" even though the pronoun refers to an individual: "Everyone went on the rides of their own choice." Grammar purists cringe at the plural pronoun with the singular antecedent but want to respect both genders.

With our modern sensibilities that take into account males and females, some people might protest when the Bible speaks of Christians' adoption as *sons*. We're likely to hear, "You mean sons and daughters, don't you?" This comes into play when the apostle Paul catalogs the riches of our redemption in Christ:

> Blessed be the God and Father of our Lord Jesus Christ, who has blessed us with every spiritual blessing in the heavenly places in Christ, just as He chose us in Him before the foundation of the world, that we should be holy and without blame before Him in love, having predestined us to *adoption as sons* by Jesus Christ to Himself, according to the good pleasure of His will, to the praise of the glory of His grace, by which He made us accepted in the Beloved. (Eph. 1:3–6, emphasis added)

God's intention for us is not merely to exonerate us from sin's guilt and condemnation. It is to adopt us as His very own children.

When the apostle describes that adoption elsewhere, he does so in terms of adoption as *sons*. Consider his explanation to the Galatians:

> But when the fullness of the time had come, God sent forth His Son, born of a woman, born under the law, to redeem those who were under the law, that we might receive the adoption as sons.
>
> And because you are sons, God has sent forth the Spirit of His Son into your hearts, crying out, "Abba, Father!" Therefore you are no longer a slave but a son, and if a son, then an heir of God through Christ. (Gal. 4:4–7)

In speaking of sons, Paul is not adhering to some grammatical form. He is not being sexist in his terms and is certainly not excluding females from God's blessings of salvation (see Gal. 3:26–29). Both men and women are children of God (see Rom. 8:14–17), but it is in *the Son*, Jesus Christ, that we count ourselves heirs as firstborn. In that day, the rights and privileges of the heir rested with the firstborn son. Jesus is both the "firstborn over all creation" (Col. 1:15) and the "firstborn from the dead" (Col. 1:18). Jesus holds the place of prominence. Those rights and privileges belong exclusively to Jesus as firstborn Son and are ours through trust in Him in our adoption as sons. We claim the Father of Jesus as our own.

After His resurrection, Jesus appeared to Mary Magdalene. Mary was grief-stricken because Jesus's body was missing from the tomb, but she did not recognize Him. When Jesus revealed Himself to her, He made this remarkable declaration: "I am ascending to My Father and your Father, and to My God and your God" (John 20:17). Imagine having the same intimacy of relationship to God as Jesus does! Yet that is precisely the case for those who are united with Jesus by faith. We can call God Father. In His High Priestly Prayer of John 17, Jesus incorporates us into an eternal fellowship that He shares with the Father, something we enjoy now and will one day enjoy more fully.

For years I went to a church where we prayed the prayer that Jesus taught His disciples to pray in the Sermon on the Mount (Matt. 6:9–13). We called it "the Our Father." Sometimes I would pray that prayer ten times in a row. Actually, it would be more accurate to say recited the prayer because I would do it mindlessly and at a pace that would rival those legal disclaimers at the end of radio advertisements. But when God captured my heart and opened my blinded eyes, that prayer took on radically new meaning in relationship to God. I took the name *Father* to my lips, delighting in all that it meant, savoring the love and grace inherent in it. It meant I had been adopted. I was a child of God, having the rights of an heir—all because of Jesus.

When the Creed refers to God as the Father almighty, it points to God the Father in eternal relationship with God the Son, and it sets us up for the next section, that of "Jesus Christ, his only Son, our Lord," in whom we are blessed as children of God and heirs of eternal life. When we recite the Creed, we do so as a family of faith, kindred spirits bound together by the blood of Jesus Christ.

I was being interviewed for a Christian radio program about one of my books. The show was live, and listeners were invited to ask questions. The book had a chapter titled "My Father, the Gardener." One listener e-mailed a question asking if God was the father of all humanity, or only of Christians. I thought it was a helpful question, particularly in view of the teaching of some churches that God is the father of all, and all humankind forms a family of God irrespective of religious belief. I gave one of those "yes and no" answers. God is the father of all people in a Creator sense. Paul said as much in his address to the philosophers at Athens: "We are indeed [God's] offspring" (Acts 17:28). Every person, regardless of religious belief, bears the image of the One who made them. So the answer is yes to God being father of all as their maker. But the answer is no to knowing God as father in a redemptive sense. Calling God Father in that way comes only through faith in Jesus Christ, in realizing the blessing of adoption. That's the thrust of Paul explaining that the evidence and goodness of a Creator is intended "that they should seek" God and "find Him" (Acts 17:27). Those who are God's offspring by virtue of creation are urged to turn to Him for salvation and so know Him as Father. That amazing promise continues to this day to all who will believe God and believe in His Son, a belief owed to the life-giving grace and power of the Holy Spirit: "But as many as received Him, to them He gave the right to become children of God, to those who believe in His name: who were born, not of blood, nor of the will of the flesh, nor of the will of man, but of God" (John 1:12–13).

Knowing God as Father comes only through faith in Jesus Christ, the One to whom the Creed now turns.

4

JESUS THE CHRIST

I believe in Jesus Christ,
his only Son, our Lord.

What does it mean to believe in Jesus Christ? It is true that there are those who are convinced that Jesus never existed, just like there are those who deny the Holocaust. It seems that their belief is driven by ideology that does not want to acknowledge historicity. But these sorts are the exception rather than the rule. Most will admit the existence of a historical Jesus. That does not mean, however, they agree with the statement of the Apostles' Creed. Perhaps the better question is not what it means to believe in Jesus Christ, but what the Creed calls us to affirm. The Apostles' Creed makes a momentous demand. It says something about the person of Jesus that is a defining declaration.

A popular game show when I was growing up was called *To Tell the Truth*. Three contenders would take their places, each claiming to be the real deal. A panel of celebrity judges would ask questions of the contenders to test their claim, and the judges would make their guesses. The big reveal would be when the emcee would ask, "Will the real mountain climber [or whatever the role was] please stand up?" The contenders would bob from their seats to build suspense until the actual mountain climber would rise from his or her seat.

When it comes to Jesus, we need to ask if He is the real Christ, the promised, prophesied, prefigured Messiah of God. The Creed leads us to affirm that Jesus is the Christ; all other contenders are pretenders. To say we believe in Jesus Christ is to make a twofold statement: first, we acknowledge that Jesus is the Messiah and there is no other; second, we profess faith in Jesus for His messianic work.

We might note that the Apostles' Creed was formulated before the great christological debates and heresies of the early church. People like Arius (fourth century) and Nestorius (fifth century) had not yet risen to challenge the deity of Christ or the nature of His being fully God and fully man in one person. As a result, the Apostles' Creed is more rustic, simply laying out basic biblical teaching.

The Christ

My last name is Gale. I come from a family of Gales. I have children that carry on the Gale name. But there is no family of Christs. Christ is not a surname. The Greek word *Christ* translates the Hebrew word *Messiah*.[1] Both *Christ* and *Messiah* mean "Anointed One," the One set apart and endued with the Spirit of God as God's promised prophet, priest, and king. All the Old Testament points to Jesus as the Messiah promised from the garden of Eden (Gen. 3:15), the One who would bring deliverance. Over the years we learn about this

---

1. Hebrew is the language of the Old Testament, while the New Testament was written in Greek.

Messiah as more and more of the Bible was written. We learn He would be a greater prophet than Moses. In fact, He would be called *the* Prophet (cf. Deut. 18:15–18 with John 1:21). He would be the perfect Priest. Remarkably, He would be *both* priest and sacrifice (Isaiah 53; Heb. 7:26–28). And He would be the ultimate King, the son in the line of David who would sit on the throne of an everlasting, redemptive kingdom (2 Sam. 7:12–16; Luke 1:30–33).

To say that Jesus is the Christ is to ascribe to Him all that the Old Testament heralded of God's Messiah. John 5 paints an epochal portrait of Jesus, speaking of His identity and the climactic character of His mission. In that chapter Jesus says this in verse 39: "You search the Scriptures, for in them you think you have eternal life; and these are they which testify of Me." The Scriptures of which He speaks are the Old Testament. After His resurrection, Jesus summarizes the message of the entire Old Testament with these words to His disciples: "Thus it is written, and thus it was necessary for the Christ to suffer and to rise from the dead the third day, and that repentance and remission of sins should be preached in His name to all nations, beginning at Jerusalem" (Luke 24:46–47). To say that Jesus is the Christ is a statement of historic proportion.

The New Testament goes to great lengths to make clear who Jesus is. John explained the purpose of his gospel account, in which he recorded remarkable signs and teaching about Jesus: "And truly Jesus did many other signs in the presence of His disciples, which are not written in this book; but these are written that you may believe that Jesus is the Christ, the Son of God, and that believing you may have life in His name" (20:30–31). Much of the New Testament aims to reveal Jesus as the Christ and persuade the readers to rest on Him for salvation. The book of Acts, which describes the message and mission of the early church, carries this emphasis by both Peter and Paul as apostles of the Lord Jesus.

> [Peter preached,] "Therefore let all the house of Israel know assuredly that God has made this Jesus, whom you crucified, both Lord and Christ." (2:36)

> Then Paul, as his custom was, went in to them, and for three Sabbaths reasoned with them from the Scriptures, explaining and demonstrating that the Christ had to suffer and rise again from the dead, and saying, "This Jesus whom I preach to you is the Christ." (17:2–3)

> For [Paul] vigorously refuted the Jews publicly, showing from the Scriptures that Jesus is the Christ. (18:28)

This Christ was not just a Savior for the Jews but for all who would believe—Jew and Gentile.

God the Father Himself bears witness to Jesus. From the start of Jesus's public ministry at His baptism at the Jordan River where the voice from heaven rang out, "This is My beloved Son, in whom I am well pleased" (Matt. 3:17) to the impending culmination of the ministry at the Mount of Transfiguration, where God's voice came out of a bright cloud "saying, 'This is My beloved Son, in whom I am well pleased. Hear Him!'" (Matt. 17:5), God the Father testifies to the identity of the Son. In addition to the entire Scripture, which bore witness to Him, Jesus urges us to hear and to heed the testimony of the Father: "Most assuredly, I say to you, he who hears My word and believes in Him who sent Me has everlasting life, and shall not come into judgment, but has passed from death into life" (John 5:24). Actually, since the word "in" is absent from the original text, it would more accurately be put, "believes Him who sent Me." Jesus urges us to believe the Father, who calls us to recognize Jesus and to believe in Jesus, resting by faith in this Messiah as the Savior of sinners.

Jesus

The Creed calls us to believe that the Christ is Jesus. Jesus was not an uncommon name in that day. In view particularly, as the Creed will make clear, is the Jesus born to Mary, the Jesus of the gospel accounts. Jesus is His given name. It means "the Lord saves." But there's more to it, as evidenced in Matthew's record of His naming:

> Now the birth of Jesus Christ was as follows: After His mother Mary was betrothed to Joseph, before they came together, she was found with child of the Holy Spirit. Then Joseph her husband, being a just man, and not wanting to make her a public example, was minded to put her away secretly. But while he thought about these things, behold, an angel of the Lord appeared to him in a dream, saying, "Joseph, son of David, do not be afraid to take to you Mary your wife, for that which is conceived in her is of the Holy Spirit. And she will bring forth a Son, and you shall call His name JESUS, for He will save His people from their sins."
>
> So all this was done that it might be fulfilled which was spoken by the Lord through the prophet, saying: "Behold, the virgin shall be with child, and bear a Son, and they shall call His name Immanuel," which is translated, "God with us."
>
> Then Joseph, being aroused from sleep, did as the angel of the Lord commanded him and took to him his wife, and did not know her till she had brought forth

her firstborn Son. And he called His name JESUS. (Matt.
1:18–25)

Clearly the name of the child carried great significance. The
name reflected His mission and connected His coming and
mission with Old Testament prophecy.

Prophetic fulfillment spoke to the legitimacy of something. It said God was in it and His word was coming true, as
foretold. When we read of Jesus being born in Bethlehem, we
connect to the prophecy the prophet Micah made about the
Messiah hundreds of years prior (Mic. 5:2). It is astounding
and convincing to read of the scores of prophesies about the
Messiah that were fulfilled in the details of Jesus's life.

But the angelic announcement of Jesus's naming presents
us with a prophetic paradox. We can think of it in terms of
probability. The odds of the child born to Mary being male
were 50/50. That He would be born of a virgin was zero,
impossible. But the one element that could be controlled
to fulfill the prophecy from Isaiah was the name. Yet the
angel tells Joseph to name the baby Jesus in fulfillment of a
prophecy that He would be named Immanuel. My father was
named Enoch. His father was named Enoch. If someone had
bet my mother and father that I would be named Enoch but
I was instead named Stanley, my parents would lose the bet
on something they controlled. How can Jesus's birth be a fulfillment of the eighth-century-BC prophecy if He was named
Jesus and not Immanuel? The gender checks out. Even being
born of a virgin checks out. But does not the prophecy fail
because of the wrong name?

In this case, we see more than a straight-line prophecy.
The angel is telling us something more about the identity

of this son born to Mary. This Child born, this Son given, who would bring forgiveness of sins (see Isaiah 53) and would establish an everlasting kingdom (see Isa. 9:6–7) is none other than God in the flesh. "Immanuel" speaks to His person—God with us. "Jesus" speaks to His mission—the Lord saves. That's what the angel is saying: this son born of a virgin is God incarnate to save. This Jesus is the Christ.

God's Only Son

We've already seen God the Father affirming Jesus as His beloved Son at both His baptism and on the Mount of Transfiguration. This credential distinguishes Jesus from every other human who has ever lived. As we've also seen, by virtue of faith in Christ, we are sons. Our sonship is a hallmark of our salvation, the apex of the panoply of blessings that are ours in Christ. But we are not sons as Jesus is. We are adopted as sons. Jesus has perpetual existence as Son in relationship to the Father. He is Son to the Father in the eternal relationship of the Trinity. That means Jesus is divine.

John lays particular emphasis on this in his gospel account. While the other gospel writers tend to stress the humanity of Christ, John wants us to see His deity. While the other accounts begin with Jesus's birth or the start of His earthly ministry, John begins with a description of the preincarnate Jesus: "In the beginning was the Word, and the Word was with God, and the Word was God…. And the Word became flesh and dwelt among us, and we beheld His glory, the glory as of the only begotten of the Father, full of grace and truth" (John 1:1, 14).

As the Son, Jesus reveals the unseen God. Paul puts it this way in his letter to the Colossians: "He is the image of the invisible God, the firstborn over all creation. For by Him all things were created that are in heaven and that are on earth, visible and invisible, whether thrones or dominions or principalities or powers. All things were created through Him and for Him. And He is before all things, and in Him all things consist" (1:15–17). John records a similar statement: "Jesus said to him, 'Have I been with you so long, and yet you have not known Me, Philip? He who has seen Me has seen the Father'" (John 14:9). Both John and Paul speak of Jesus as God present with us, not part of the creation He has made.

There are some people who insist that Jesus is not God. After all, doesn't He pray to God and doesn't He make reference to a Father distinct from Himself? But this insistence reflects incomplete understanding of God's self-revelation in the Bible. It confuses the eternal person of God the Son with the humanity of God incarnate. Those who try to make a case for Jesus not being divine will point us to passages of the Bible that show the humanity of Christ while neglecting those passages that demonstrate the divinity of Christ. But the accounts make it clear that Jesus is God. For example, Jesus receives worship. Only God is to be worshiped. Jesus forgives sin. Only God is able to forgive sin. When Jesus forgave the sins of a paralyzed man, the Jewish leaders rightly understood: "Why does this Man speak blasphemies like this? Who can forgive sins but God alone?" (Mark 2:7). In conversation with these leaders Jesus said, "My Father has been working until now, and I have been working" (John 5:17). Again, the message was clear, as John records: "Therefore the Jews sought all the more to kill Him, because He not only broke the Sabbath, but also said that God was His Father, making Himself equal with God" (John 5:18).

Jesus also claimed for Himself attributes and titles that belong only to God. Note this spirited exchange. It begins with a question from the Jews:

"Are You greater than our father Abraham, who is dead? And the prophets are dead. Who do You make Yourself out to be?"

Jesus answered, "If I honor Myself, My honor is nothing. It is My Father who honors Me, of whom you say that He is your God. Yet you have not known Him, but I know Him. And if I say, 'I do not know Him,' I shall be a liar like you; but I do know Him and keep His word. Your father Abraham rejoiced to see My day, and he saw it and was glad."

Then the Jews said to Him, "You are not yet fifty years old, and have You seen Abraham?"

Jesus said to them, "Most assuredly, I say to you, before Abraham was, I AM." (John 8:53–58)

The Jews wanted to kill Jesus for blasphemy. I AM was the name by which God revealed Himself to Moses at the burning bush in Exodus 3, a name unique to Him. Jesus was asserting His divine being, eternal and inherent. He was saying that He is God. He preexisted Moses and Abraham.

Another evidence of the deity of Jesus is found in scriptural exposition. A clear example is in the New Testament book of Hebrews. The writer of the book goes to great pains to explain Jesus as the promised Messiah and considers particularly how the Old Testament sacrificial system is fulfilled in the work of Jesus as both priest and sacrifice. The first two chapters of the book lay out the person of Christ, with chapter 1 stressing His deity and chapter 2 His humanity. The opening verses speak of Jesus as the Son of God. He is distinct from the Father, but He is distinguished as God: "God, who at various times and in various ways spoke in time past to the fathers by the prophets, has in these last days spoken to us by His Son, whom He has appointed heir of all things, through whom also He made the worlds; who [is] the brightness of His glory and the express image of His person" (Heb. 1:1–3).

Then the author of Hebrews brings Old Testament verses to bear, calling for worship of the Son, something only God is to receive. "But when He again brings the firstborn into the world, He says: 'Let all the angels of God worship Him'" (1:6). The icing on the cake is found in what comes next when God says to the Son: "Your throne, O God, is forever and ever; a scepter of righteousness is the scepter of Your kingdom" (1:8).

So Jesus as the only Son of God is a clear reference to Christ's deity. But when we make that declaration with the Creed, we say something more. Jesus is not only the Son; He is the Son *given*, sent for us and for our salvation. An Old Testament preview is found in the book of Genesis where Abraham is told to offer his son Isaac on the altar of sacrifice. Observe the language: "Then [God] said, 'Take now your son, your only son Isaac, whom you love, and go to the land of Moriah, and offer him there as a burnt offering on one of the mountains of which I shall tell you'" (Gen. 22:2). Isaac is identified as Abraham's *only* son, whom he *loves*. Abraham was spared that awful sacrifice, and Isaac was spared that ultimate sacrifice. But at Mount Moriah many years later, God would give His only Son, whom He loves, and would not spare Him but offer Him up as a sacrifice: "For God so loved the world that He gave His only begotten Son, that whoever believes in Him should not perish but have everlasting life" (John 3:16).

What that means is that in Jesus, God Himself—God in the flesh—is with us to accomplish a salvation only He could achieve. The faith called for in the Apostles' Creed understands Jesus as the Son of God, beloved of the Father, given to die for sinners in their place. One final title is ascribed to the Jesus the Creed calls us to believe in. He is Christ. He is God's only Son. And He is Lord.

Our Lord

Lord can be used as a title of deference in the Bible, and not just of Jesus. Sometimes it simply means "sir." For example, when a Roman military officer approached Jesus to ask Him to heal his servant, he addresses Him this way: "Lord, if You are willing, You can make me clean" (Matt. 8:2). We want to ascribe no meaning to *lord* beyond an expression of respect. When Paul and Silas were imprisoned in Philippi, the jailer addressed them as lords: "Sirs, what must I do to be saved?" (Acts 16:30). But there are those instances where the title *lord* clearly carries great, even momentous, significance, such as we saw above in Peter's address at Pentecost: "Therefore let all the house of Israel know assuredly that God has made this Jesus, whom you crucified, both Lord and Christ" (Acts 2:36). It is in this latter sense that we understand Jesus in the Creed.

At the close of Matthew's gospel account, Jesus issues an order: "Go therefore and make disciples of all the nations, baptizing them in the name of the Father and of the Son and of the Holy Spirit, teaching them to observe all things that I have commanded you" (Matt. 28:19–20). The "therefore" of that commission flows from a game-changing declaration: "All authority has been given to Me in heaven and on earth"

(Matt. 28:18). Certainly that authority related to Jesus commanding His disciples, but it had to do with much, much more. The apostle Paul gives an idea of the scope and nature of this authority in his letter to the Ephesians. We step into the flow of a prayer by Paul:

> And what is the exceeding greatness of His power toward us who believe, according to the working of His mighty power which He worked in Christ when He raised Him from the dead and seated Him at His right hand in the heavenly places, far above all principality and power and might and dominion, and every name that is named, not only in this age but also in that which is to come.
>
> And He put all things under His feet, and gave Him to be head over all things to the church, which is His body, the fullness of Him who fills all in all. (1:19–23)

The authority in view in establishing Jesus Christ as Lord is a *kingdom* authority. The angel Gabriel testified to this authority in his announcement to Mary about the child to be born of her: "He will be great, and will be called the Son of the Highest; and the Lord God will give Him the throne of His father David. And He will reign over the house of Jacob forever, and of His kingdom there will be no end" (Luke 1:32–33). This kingdom would stand in contrast to the kingdoms of this fallen world. Unlike the kingdoms of human history that rise and fall, this kingdom would never end. It will be the kingdom of God and His Christ, a kingdom of righteousness, peace, and joy—a redemptive kingdom.

As God, Jesus has always been king, absolute sovereign over all He has made. But while Jesus has always been king in a creation sense, He has not always been king in a redemptive sense. It is by His incarnation, death, resurrection, and ascension that He achieved His kingdom mission and so is made both Lord and Christ. For Jesus to be Lord means that He has ushered in the kingdom that He spoke so much about in the gospel accounts. He would often introduce His parables with the expression, "The kingdom is like...."

So when we speak in the Creed of Jesus as Lord, we recognize Him in His redemptive victory and kingdom authority. Moreover, we not only acknowledge Him as such, we pledge allegiance to Him, heeding the call found in Romans:

> If you confess with your mouth the Lord Jesus and believe in your heart that God has raised Him from the dead, you will be saved. For with the heart one believes unto righteousness, and with the mouth confession is made unto salvation. For the Scripture says, "Whoever believes on Him will not be put to shame." For there is no distinction between Jew and Greek, for the same Lord over all is rich to all who call upon Him. For "whoever calls on the name of the LORD shall be saved." (10:9–13)

To affirm Jesus as Lord is not merely an act of respect and not even an expression of servant to master; it is to bow the knee before Jesus in trust and commitment to His kingdom.

To call Him "our" Lord is to align ourselves with others of kindred faith and count ourselves among the kingdom community of the people of God, confessing the crucified, now risen Jesus for salvation. Paul describes this recognition:

> And being found in appearance as a man, He humbled Himself and became obedient to the point of death, even the death of the cross. Therefore God also has highly exalted Him and given Him the name which is above every name, that at the name of Jesus every knee

should bow, of those in heaven, and of those on earth, and of those under the earth, and that every tongue should confess that Jesus Christ is Lord, to the glory of God the Father. (Phil. 2:8–11)

God the Father almighty has given His Son and bestowed on Him kingdom authority. Our confession of Him as Lord brings glory to the Father and to the Son.

A Kingdom Creed

In embracing the Apostles' Creed, we distinguish ourselves as Christians. In so doing, we distance ourselves from others. Jews can say they believe in Jesus, in the sense that they admit the existence of Jesus. Josephus, the first-century Jewish historian, spoke of "a wise man called Jesus, and his conduct was good and he was known to be virtuous. Many people among the Jews and the other nations became his disciples. Pilate condemned him to be crucified and to die."[2]

Josephus, as a Jew and historian, acknowledges the historicity of Jesus. Non-Jewish historians also believe in Jesus as a person who existed at a time in human history. In fact, many regard Him as a good man, wise teacher, and wonderful model for selfless living, lumping Him in with enlightened visionaries like Martin Luther King Jr. and Mahatma Gandhi. Muslims also believe in the existence of Jesus and give Him special prominence as a prophet of God, second only to Muhammad. Jesus is even mentioned in the Qur'an. The devil himself believes in Jesus. Episodes are recorded in the Bible in which Satan encountered Jesus and demons recognized Him.

---

2. Josephus, *Antiquities*, in *Josephus: The Essential Works*, ed. and trans. Paul L. Maier (Grand Rapids: Kregel, 1994), 18:63.

Things change, however, when we go on to say, "I believe in Jesus Christ, his only Son." We lose the Jews. They neither believe that Jesus is the Christ nor the Son of God. While many Jews, including the apostles, embraced Jesus, the Jewish faith rejects the idea that Jesus is the Christ and still looks for the Messiah to come. We lose the Muslims. The Qur'an explicitly denies the deity of Christ. But we don't lose Satan. He is still on board, seeing Jesus as the Son of God. From the mouth of demons comes this confession: "I know who You are—the Holy One of God!" (Luke 4:34).

But when we declare that we believe "in Jesus Christ, his only Son, our Lord," we distance ourselves from Satan and his minions as well. The Greek language has two words for "in" that make a distinction hard to capture in English. To believe in Jesus for salvation is to believe "into," like the surrendering dive of faith that immerses its trust fully into the living water that is Jesus Christ. So to believe into Jesus is to bow the knee before Him as the Lord of lords and King of kings. It is to recognize His authority and give Him our allegiance, purposing to honor and obey Him, to render unto Him dominion and power and glory forever. Satan believes in Jesus but does not believe into Jesus to salvation.

There is one other group from which we separate ourselves with a profession of faith in the Christ of the Creed. Our land is filled with people who consider themselves Christians who even recite the words of the Creed when they attend church. But they know not the One they confess. I say this not to judge people's hearts. Only God can do that. I say this to account for what Jesus Himself says: "Not everyone who says to Me, 'Lord, Lord,' shall enter the kingdom of heaven, but he who does the will of My Father in heaven. Many will say to Me in that day, 'Lord, Lord, have we not prophesied in Your name, cast out demons in Your name, and done many wonders in Your name?' And then I will declare to them, 'I never knew you; depart from Me, you who practice lawlessness!'" (Matt. 7:21–23; see also the scene at the final judgment in Matt. 25:41–46). There are those who call Christ Lord, and not just in the sense of respect. They call Him Lord in acknowledgment of who He is, but not in the embrace of saving faith.

Theologians of yesteryear had categories for such folks. They distinguished between professors of faith and possessors of faith. Professors counted themselves among the people of God in a faith that was merely religious. But possessors embraced Christ with a heart of faith worked by the Spirit of God, saving faith. Jesus illustrates the difference in the parable of the soils (Mark 4:1–20), in which two soils (rocky and thorny) produce plants that appear to have life but die away because they have no roots. Only the good soil given by God's grace and power produces plants that will multiply and endure to the glory of God.

In a parable of the kingdom, Jesus described the field of those who profess Christianity as filled with wheat and weeds (Matt. 13:24–30). Wheat are the possessors of faith; weeds, the mere professors. Though both wheat and weeds are permitted to remain in the field of the visible church, what we might see on a church roll or gathered on a Sunday morning, there will come a day when they will be separated at the harvest of the final judgment: "Let both grow together until the harvest, and at the time of harvest I will say to the reapers, 'First gather together the tares and bind them in bundles to burn them, but gather the wheat into my barn'" (Matt. 13:30).

Knowing that there are professors of faith in the church today, the Apostles' Creed serves the dual function of evangelizing the weeds and edifying the wheat in preparation for the kingdom to come. Those who in saving faith embrace the Christ of the Creed will be part of the eternal kingdom of God and His Christ. Those who refuse to own Him as Lord will find themselves part of the kingdom of this world that will be destroyed (see Rev. 12:9–11; 20:9–15).

5

BORN, BLED, AND BURIED

I believe in Jesus Christ… who was
conceived by the Holy Spirit and born of the virgin Mary.
He suffered under Pontius Pilate,
was crucified, died, and was buried;
he descended to hell.

The Creed now shifts from Christ's person to His mission. If belief in Jesus as the Christ of God, the Son of God, and the Lord announced by God gives us the grand scheme, the remainder of the second section of the Creed presents the boots-on-the-ground picture. It walks us through the various features of Jesus's life in His humanity that qualify Him as the Messiah sufficient for our salvation. While the Apostles' Creed does not give us a technical explanation of Jesus as sinless, sacrificial substitute, it does lead us from His birth in humility to His return in glory in His role as representative of those He came to save.

Born

Soldiers heading into battle do not wear their dress whites. Rather, they are outfitted with combat gear appropriate for mission, suitable to the environment in which the warfare is to be waged.

Like a combat soldier, Jesus came on a mission. His mission was announced way back in the garden of Eden, right in the thick of the catastrophe that made the mission necessary. In the garden God addressed the serpent, a representation of Satan (see Rev. 20:2):

> And I will put enmity
> Between you and the woman,
> And between your seed and her Seed;
> He shall bruise your head,
> And you shall bruise His heel. (Gen. 3:15)

The *seed* of the woman refers to an offspring, a baby to be born on a mission from God to confront and conquer Satan.[1] Jesus is that promised Seed. His mission is described in combat terms. He would wage a battle that only He could fight. Throughout the Old Testament, we come to understand this promised Deliverer through various portraits and prophesies, until He emerges on the scene of human history to engage the enemy of our souls.

Just as soldiers need the proper equipment for their mission, so Jesus as the eternal Son of God needed outfitting for His task. The writer of Hebrews explains both the mission and the provision for it:

---

1. For more detail on the nature of Christ's battle with Satan and what that means for us in our salvation and in our daily lives, see Stanley D. Gale, *Warfare Witness: Contending with Spiritual Opposition in Everyday Evangelism* (Fearn, Ross-shire, Scotland: Christian Focus, 2005); and Stanley D. Gale, *What Is Spiritual Warfare?*, Basics of the Faith (Phillipsburg, N.J.: P&R, 2008).

> Inasmuch then as the children have partaken of flesh and blood, He Himself likewise shared in the same, that through death He might destroy him who had the power of death, that is, the devil, and release those who through fear of death were all their lifetime subject to bondage. For indeed He does not give aid to angels, but He does give aid to the seed of Abraham. Therefore, in all things He had to be made like His brethren, that He might be a merciful and faithful High Priest in things pertaining to God, to make propitiation for the sins of the people. (2:14–17)

In view is the adversary—the devil—and Christ's outfitting for the nature of the battle. The eternal Son of God took on true and full humanity so that He could represent the people He came to deliver and suffer in their place. He would need a flesh-and-blood body to do that, and not just a human shell but humanity in every sense of the term, including intellect, emotions, and whatever else makes us human.

The writer of Hebrews calls our attention to two things about Jesus's body. One, the body that Jesus took on was not like that of the angels. The reason is that Jesus did not come to represent angels as their substitute. Sometimes we'll hear the sentiment that believers become angels in heaven. It's a good thing that's not true because Jesus did not come to redeem fallen angels. He came to redeem fallen humans by being made like them in humanity to represent them. Two, Jesus did come to represent human beings, but not all human beings. He came to deliver the seed of Abraham. That expression should bring to our mind not just Jews, but Jews and Gentiles (Rom. 9:6–8; Gal. 3:7–9) or, as Paul put it, the seed of Abraham (see Gal. 3:16). In one sense that seed is believers, but in its fullest sense that Seed was Jesus Christ. God's plan from the beginning included one Seed, one Savior, one salvation for Jew and non-Jew alike (see Gen. 12:3; Rom. 1:16–17), for all who would believe in Him. For the writer of Hebrews to mention Abraham speaks to the special relationship called *covenant* that grows from the seed of promise throughout the entire Old Testament and comes to full bloom in the person and work of Jesus Christ.

In order to carry out His mission of salvation, which the Apostles' Creed unfolds for us, the Son of God needed to be clothed with humanity. The writer of Hebrews highlights that body in quoting from the Old Testament (Ps. 40:6–8). He shows the inadequacy of animal sacrifice to take away our sin as fallen people and deliver us from the clutches of Satan:

> For it is not possible that the blood of bulls and goats could take away sins.

> Therefore, when He came into the world, He said:
> "Sacrifice and offering You did not desire,
> But a body You have prepared for Me.
> In burnt offerings and sacrifices for sin
> You had no pleasure.
> Then I said, 'Behold, I have come—
> In the volume of the book it is written of Me—
> To do Your will, O God.'" (10:4–7)

The will of God was to give His only Son as a sacrifice and substitute (see Isa. 53:4–6, 10) for undeserving sinners. For Jesus to be able to be that sacrifice and substitute He needed authentic and complete humanity.

The Creed goes on to declare *how* Jesus as eternal God was made human. Jesus's birth was ordinary, in the sense that it was something an obstetrician would have experienced many times. His conception, however, was anything but ordinary. The Bible records that Jesus was conceived by the Holy Spirit in the womb of Mary while she was still a virgin. Luke gives us a record of how God alerted Mary to a pregnancy like no other:

> Now in the sixth month the angel Gabriel was sent by God to a city of Galilee named Nazareth, to a virgin betrothed to a man whose name was Joseph, of the house of David. The virgin's name was Mary. And having come in, the angel said to her, "Rejoice, highly favored one, the Lord is with you; blessed are you among women!"
>
> But when she saw him, she was troubled at his saying, and considered what manner of greeting this was. Then the angel said to her, "Do not be afraid, Mary, for you have found favor with God. And behold, you will conceive in your womb and bring forth a Son, and shall call His name Jesus." (1:26–31)

Mary, no doubt incredulous, asked of the angel: "How can this be, since I do not know a man?" (v. 34). In other words, Mary was a virgin. She had not known a man in the biblical sense of sexual intercourse. How could she possibly be with child? The angel answered her: "The Holy Spirit will come upon you, and the power of the Highest will overshadow you" (v. 35).

When the angel appeared to Joseph, Mary's betrothed, to bring him into the loop, the celestial messenger explained in terms of Old Testament prophecy that "the virgin shall be with child" (Matt. 1:23). Joseph would be the dad, but he would not be the father. Rather than Matthew designating him as the father of Jesus, as he had designated all the other men in the genealogy that opens the chapter, Matthew identifies him as "the husband of Mary, of whom was born Jesus" (Matt. 1:16).

Clearly Jesus's conception carries great significance to qualify Him for the sin-bearing and sinner-saving mission for which He came into this world. But what makes it so significant that it warrants emphasis in the Apostles' Creed?

Jesus's conception was unlike any other. We find records of barren women getting pregnant, like Sarah (Gen. 18:9–11; 21:1–2) and Hannah (1 Sam. 1:19–20), attesting to the power of God to open the womb and to give life. But never do we find a woman becoming pregnant without male involvement. Even the prophecy in Isaiah that the angel mentions to Joseph is not fulfilled in Isaiah's day by a virgin. History would wait until the fullness of time, when God would send His Son to be born of a woman who was a virgin (Gal. 4:4). In respect to procreation, God had performed the miracle of miracles. The Holy Spirit Himself had caused Mary to be with child. Not that we want to parse the conception of Jesus in biological terms, but we do want to see the uniqueness of Jesus as God the Son, taking on developing humanity like any other, in the womb of Mary.

Why was it necessary that Jesus be born of a virgin? It was not because the sexual act itself is sinful, or because the fallen sinful nature is passed on by the male, or because Mary was without sin and so a pure vessel for the Christ. Rather, the virgin birth accomplished three things. As Matthew pointed out, it was a prophetic pointer to the Messiah. When a virgin conceived and bore a son, that was a telltale sign of the fulfillment of prophecy. The child was both Immanuel (God with us) and Jesus (the Lord saves)—God incarnate to save. Second, taking on human nature allowed the eternal

Son of God to be fully God and fully man in one person. He was the God-man. Finally, through supernatural conception, Jesus was equipped to stand in the place of human beings as the sinless substitute. Jesus was unique in His qualification as the Christ of God.

The Bible teaches that everyone naturally descended from Adam carries the contamination and condemnation of sin. The apostle Paul explains this in Romans 5:12. Adam represented the entire human race, even to the degree that this can be said: "Therefore, just as through one man sin entered the world, and death through sin, and thus death spread to all men, because all sinned." Sin, original sin, accompanies all those born into this world. It is not that the male is the sin carrier, like one would pass on a defective gene. Rather, the issue is being a descendent of Adam by ordinary means.

Jesus, however, was born without original sin. While every human is born in sin, sin is not part of humanity. It is part of *fallen* humanity. Jesus was uniquely conceived. He was born without a sin nature, beginning with His conception. So Jesus was truly human—and in a sense no one else can claim since He was born without the infection of sin. Our humanity is true but corrupted. Jesus was the perfect human. His sinlessness was not owed to anything about Mary, as though she were a sinless vessel. In fact, Mary herself acknowledged her need of a Savior and thus her sin condition (see Luke 1:46–47).[2] Of all her children (Matt. 13:53–56), only Jesus

---

2. Certainly Mary is blessed among women (Luke 1:42) in that she was the chosen vessel of the Messiah, something Jewish women throughout the years longed to be, beginning with Eve herself. But as one blessed, Mary was not to be revered. We can see this inappropriate veneration of Mary budding even in Jesus's day, something rebuked by Jesus:

would be conceived supernaturally because of all her children, only one would be God's Messiah, the incarnation of the Son of God.

While we don't want to enter into a technical discussion about how the deity and the humanity of Jesus fit together, as the early church fathers did in considering the Nicene Creed, we do want to fully affirm that the Apostles' Creed recognizes the full and true deity of Christ and the full and true humanity of Christ, two natures in one person. One passage of Scripture that helps us see the deity and humanity of Jesus provides an illustration about humility and deference to others:

> Let each of you look out not only for his own interests, but also for the interests of others.
>
> Let this mind be in you which was also in Christ Jesus, who, being in the form of God, did not consider it robbery to be equal with God, but made Himself of no reputation, taking the form of a bondservant, and coming in the likeness of men. And being found in appearance as a man, He humbled Himself and became obedient to the point of death, even the death of the cross. Therefore God also has highly exalted Him and given Him the name which is above every name, that at the name of Jesus every knee should bow, of those in heaven, and of those on earth, and of those under the earth, and that every tongue should confess that Jesus Christ is Lord, to the glory of God the Father. (Phil. 2:4–11)

And it happened, as He spoke these things, that a certain woman from the crowd raised her voice and said to Him, "Blessed is the womb that bore You, and the breasts which nursed You!"

But He said, "More than that, blessed are those who hear the word of God and keep it!" (Luke 11:27–28)

Jesus—God the Son, full of glory, the Creator, deserving of all honor and praise—laid aside His due and vested Himself with our created humanity so that He could represent us and take upon Himself the punishment for our sin. The Christmas carol expresses it eloquently:

> Christ, by highest heaven adored,
> Christ, the everlasting Lord!
> Late in time behold him come,
> Offspring of the Virgin's womb.
> Veiled in flesh the Godhead see;
> Hail th'incarnate Deity,
> Pleased as man with men to dwell,
> Jesus our Emmanuel.[3]

Those who sing that hymn confess with one voice the miracle of Jesus as God incarnate, fitted to save His people from their sins.

Bled

Christian songs must sound awfully strange to people outside the Christian faith—all this talk about blood. One popular hymn speaks of a fountain filled with blood. The first stanza goes like this:

> There is a fountain filled with blood,
> Drawn from Immanuel's veins;
> And sinners, plunged beneath that flood,
> Lose all their guilty stains.[4]

3. Charles Wesley, "Hark! the Herald Angels Sing," in the public domain.
4. William Cowper, "There Is a Fountain Filled with Blood," in the public domain. You can read the rest of the verses at https://hymnary.org/text/there_is_a_fountain_filled_with_blood_dr.

It all sounds rather gruesome, even ghoulish. The image of children playing in a fountain in a city square on a sweltering day comes to mind: blood everywhere, spraying, flowing; children splashing in it, dripping with it. But that blood of Christ has been the source of comfort and assurance for Christians throughout the ages. In fact, the eighteenth-century writer of these hymn lyrics, William Cowper, wrote this and other hymns at the counsel of his friend John Newton to help him delight in Christ and ease the depression that had prompted his suicide attempts. It was the blood of Christ that gave Cowper solace, hope, and encouragement. You might want to look up the remainder of "There Is a Fountain Filled with Blood" to read the story of love and joy that nourished Cowper's soul so weighed down with cares.

What is all this talk about blood in Christian circles? The blood of Christ did not have magical properties. Only the stuff of legends sends the intrepid explorer on an adventure to find a holy grail filled with Christ's blood to drink so that he can gain eternal life. Christ's blood is not an elixir of life. But didn't Jesus say that His blood is true drink (John 6:55), and didn't He say this: "Most assuredly, I say to you, unless you eat the flesh of the Son of Man and drink His blood, you have no life in you. Whoever eats My flesh and drinks My blood has eternal life, and I will raise him up at the last day" (John 6:53–54)?

Blood refers to life. The shedding of blood speaks not of bloodletting but of death. Had Jesus bled only from the wounds He received from His scourging and pierced hands and feet, salvation would not have been accomplished. Another hymn writer makes the connection between blood and death: "Alas, and did my Savior bleed, and did my Sovereign die!"[5] The teaching of the Bible, the good news of Christ's saving work, is that Jesus poured out His life unto death.

But the Apostles' Creed takes us to the death of Jesus by a particular route—namely, His suffering under Pontius Pilate and His being crucified. Why is Pontius Pilate mentioned by name in the Creed? Why are we told not just that Jesus suffered but that He suffered at the hand of this Roman governor? Certainly suffering is a significant component of God the Son coming into this world. Suffering characterized His mission as He entered a world filled with sin and in rebellion against God. Old Testament passages describe Jesus as God's Suffering Servant (Isaiah 42, 49, 53). In his first letter, the apostle Peter highlights Christ's suffering on the road to His death (3:18) and describes the intensity of Christ's suffering (2:21–24). But what is so significant about the suffering Jesus endured *under Pontius Pilate*?

Naming the Roman governor locates the suffering and death of Jesus at a certain point in history (AD 26–36). We do want to be reminded that what Jesus accomplished actually occurred in time and space as historical happenings. The mention of Pilate also helps us to understand how crucifixion became Jesus's means of death. The Jews did not have the authority to impose capital punishment, let alone to employ crucifixion to fulfill biblical prophecy (Deut. 21:22; Gal. 3:13).

But the primary reason for the specific mention of Pontius Pilate in the movement from conception to death likely has to do with the qualification of Jesus to bear the sin of those He came to save. Pilate served as a civil judge. The Jews

---

5. Isaac Watts, "Alas, and Did My Savior Bleed," in the public domain.

were accusing Jesus of all sorts of things, from blasphemy to treason. In his judicial capacity, Pilate examined Jesus and made this declaration: "I find no fault in Him" (John 19:6). In legal proceedings, Jesus was declared not guilty and would be sentenced to death as an explicitly innocent man.

This judicial charade highlights Jesus's blameless life. Not only did He not break Roman law, He never broke God's law—not in thought, word, or deed; not in sins committed by action or sins committed by neglect, either intentionally or unintentionally. He was the spotless Lamb of God, come to take away the sins of the world. He arrived at the cross without His own debt of sin that He might stand in the place of sinners laden with the debt of sin, the Guiltless One for the guilty ones. A hymn written by a man aptly named Bliss captures the scene:

> Bearing shame and scoffing rude,
> In my place condemned He stood,
> Sealed my pardon with His blood:
> Hallelujah, what a Savior!

> Guilty, vile, and helpless, we,
> Spotless Lamb of God was He;
> Full redemption—can it be?
> Hallelujah, what a Savior![6]

Jesus's suffering under Pontius Pilate highlights His unjust accusation and condemnation.

Having referenced Pilate, the Creed goes on to say that Jesus was crucified, the Roman government's method of choice for executing those who committed capital crimes.

---

6. Philip P. Bliss, "Man of Sorrows—What a Name," in the public domain.

Crucifixion was a particularly horrible way to die, but as horrific as Jesus's physical agony was, it paled in comparison to the agony of soul he endured. The whole biblical framework gives context for the impact of Jesus's death. The writer of Hebrews speaks of the temple and the sacrificial system of the Old Testament as previews for the sacrifice to come, looking to Jesus as both *the* effective Priest and *the* effective Sacrifice: "For such a High Priest was fitting for us, who is holy, harmless, undefiled, separate from sinners, and has become higher than the heavens; who does not need daily, as those high priests, to offer up sacrifices, first for His own sins and then for the people's, for this He did once for all when He offered up Himself" (7:26–27).

Jesus went to the cross as the sacrifice to deal with sin's debt. He atoned for sin's guilt and suffered the penalty demanded by God's justice, not just by death but by death on a cross. In his letter to the Galatians Paul writes: "Christ has redeemed us from the curse of the law, having become a curse for us (for it is written, 'Cursed is everyone who hangs on a tree')" (3:13). The reference Paul makes to a tree is found in the Old Testament and speaks to the just punishment of one who breaks God's law. Jesus, however, became accursed that we who proclaim the Creed in faith might know the blessings of His obedience in our place.

Christ's saving work is testimony to the Father's love and wisdom. In answer to the question, Who killed Jesus? the ultimate answer is not Judas, who betrayed Him; not the Jews who conspired against Him; not the mob that chose Barabbas over Jesus for release; and not Pilate, who gave Him in His innocence over to death. The answer is not even us as sinners, although our sin is certainly at issue. The ultimate answer for who killed Jesus is God Himself, as prophetic word makes clear:

> Yet it pleased the LORD to bruise Him;
> He has put Him to grief.
> When You make His soul an offering for sin,
> He shall see His seed, He shall prolong His days,
> And the pleasure of the LORD shall prosper in
>   His hand. (Isa. 53:10)

The English Standard Version puts it this way: "It was the will of the LORD to crush him." While there may be secondary causes, the primary cause of Christ's death was the will of God. It was not our sin that held Jesus to the cross; it was the redeeming love of God (John 3:16; Rom. 5:8–9) and the love of Christ for His bride, the church (Eph. 5:25).

Buried

Why is burial even mentioned? It would seem a forgone conclusion. Someone dies; that person is buried. But the Creed gives it mention because the Bible gives it special mention. In a summary of Christ's saving work, the apostle Paul says this: "For I delivered to you first of all that which I also received: that Christ died for our sins according to the Scriptures, and that He was buried, and that He rose again the third day according to the Scriptures" (1 Cor. 15:3–4). Burial signifies the reality of death.

When we think of burial, our minds might go to the funerals we have attended, culminating with the committal at graveside, where a casket is lowered into the ground. But Jesus was not buried in the ground. Rather, He was entombed. His grave was a cave in which His body was laid to rest. Matthew describes the burial of Jesus in this way: "Now when evening had come, there came a rich man from Arimathea, named Joseph, who himself had also become a disciple of Jesus. This man went to Pilate and asked for the body of Jesus. Then Pilate commanded the body to be given to him. When Joseph had taken the body, he wrapped it in a clean linen cloth, and laid it in his new tomb which he had hewn out of the rock; and he rolled a large stone against the door of the tomb, and departed" (27:57–61).

In his sermon at Pentecost, Peter sets the stage for Christ's resurrection by paralleling His death and burial to King David's one thousand years prior:

> For David says concerning Him:
>
> "I foresaw the LORD always before my face,
> For He is at my right hand, that I may not be shaken.
> Therefore my heart rejoiced, and my tongue was glad;
> Moreover my flesh also will rest in hope.
> For You will not leave my soul in Hades,
> Nor will You allow Your Holy One to see corruption.
> You have made known to me the ways of life;
> You will make me full of joy in Your presence."
>
> Men and brethren, let me speak freely to you of the patriarch David, that he is both dead and buried, and his tomb is with us to this day. Therefore, being a prophet, and knowing that God had sworn with an oath to him that of the fruit of his body, according to the flesh, He would raise up the Christ to sit on his throne, he, foreseeing this, spoke concerning the resurrection of the Christ, that His soul was not left in Hades, nor did His flesh see corruption. (Acts 2:25–31)

While Christ's burial is paralleled with David's, His resurrection is unparalleled. We'll explore the resurrection of the body when we get to that section of the Creed, but Christ's burial sets the stage for His bodily resurrection from the grave, and it anticipates our bodily resurrection from the grave. The Apostles' Creed affirms the reality of Christ's death and entombment of His body.

The Creed concludes the downward descent of Christ from glory to grave with one final, much-debated phrase. Jesus "descended to hell." This phrase was not original to the Apostles' Creed and may have been included even centuries later. Why did the church fathers think that phrase important to the gospel story? It has to do with the humanity of Jesus in His representation of us in the death we experience.

What happens when we die? We are separated body and soul. Our bodies rest in the grave until Jesus returns in glory, whereupon we are given resurrection bodies like Jesus had (1 Cor. 15:12–56; 1 Thess. 4:13–18). What happened when Jesus in His humanity died? Like us, He was separated body and soul. The Old Testament place of the departed was called Sheol. The New Testament equivalent is Hades, sometimes translated "hell." Hades does not refer to a place of punishment; that would be Gehenna, also translated "hell." Rather, the Creed references Hades to describe the human experience of death. Jesus did not enter Gehenna to be punished for the sins He bore. It was on the cross that He endured the fullness of God's wrath as He suffered the penalty of the lawbreaker and the just wrath of God in condemnation for the sins of others.

The writer of Hebrews reminds us of the judgment that awaits every human being at his or her death. "[Jesus] then would have had to suffer often since the foundation of the world; but now, once at the end of the ages, He has appeared to put away sin by the sacrifice of Himself. And as it is appointed for men to die once, but after this the judgment, so Christ was offered once to bear the sins of many. To those who eagerly wait for Him He will appear a second time, apart from sin, for salvation" (9:26–28). Men die once and face judgment. The God-man died once and faced judgment, just as those He came to represent. But, as we will see, the grave could not hold Him. The resurrection is a verdict on Jesus's own guilt or innocence. The ultimate Judge declared Jesus not guilty.

The phrase "descended to hell" belongs to the progression of the Creed and the representative work of Jesus Christ in which we find our salvation. Jesus did not go to hell to be punished or to enter into some netherworld prison to preach the gospel and interact somehow with those long dead. Rather, as Peter suggests in his sermon at Pentecost, Jesus died as David did. But death would not be the final answer, either for Him or for those He came to save. Jesus's physical body would not suffer decay as David's did. Instead, He would be raised in victory—His and all those who trust in Him. The Creed goes on to declare the rest of the story.

6

RISEN, REIGNING, RETURNING

The third day he rose again from the dead.
He ascended to heaven and is seated
at the right hand of God the Father almighty.
From there he will come to judge the living and the dead.

Magicians are a fantastical lot. I attended a show with my son at a local college campus. The audience was mesmerized and confounded by seemingly unexplainable feats of prestidigitation and misdirection. Harry Houdini, who popularized the trade, set a high bar for illusion that he continually elevated, leaving his compatriots trying to close the gap. In one trick, his arms and legs would be shackled, his body placed in a locked trunk, and the whole be submerged under water. The success of that endeavor depended on whether he emerged from what could be a watery grave.

The success of Jesus's mission also depended on whether He would emerge from the grave or whether death would hold Him. Unlike Houdini, however, Christ's triumph was not an illusion; it was a verdict, a validation, even a vindication of His work for the salvation of sinners. There were those at the time of Jesus and to this day who deny that Jesus was raised bodily from the dead. They search for some logical explanation, in large part because they refuse to believe in anything supernatural. Some suggest that Jesus did not actually die on the cross; He merely swooned and the coolness of the tomb revived Him. Others suggest some sort of conspiracy such as the one recorded in Matthew's gospel:

> Now while they were going, behold, some of the guard came into the city and reported to the chief priests all the things that had happened. When they had assembled with the elders and consulted together, they gave a large sum of money to the soldiers, saying, "Tell them, 'His disciples came at night and stole Him away while we slept.' And if this comes to the governor's ears, we will appease him and make you secure." So they took the money and did as they were instructed; and this saying is commonly reported among the Jews until this day. (28:11–15)

Some people say that Jesus rose spiritually, not physically. But the reality of Jesus's death and the actuality of His bodily resurrection are essential to the Christian faith. I have spoken with those who say that it's not important that Jesus rose from the dead. It's the thought that counts, the symbolism. The biblical record begs to differ.

The accounts of the four Gospels—Matthew, Mark, Luke, and John—do not end with Christ's death. While they make clear that Jesus did die, they relate the rest of the story. Jesus Himself summarized His mission several times, ending not on a note of defeat but of victory: "From that time Jesus began to show to His disciples that He must go to Jerusalem, and suffer many things from the elders and chief priests and scribes, and be killed, and be raised the third day" (Matt.

16:21). In recounting the events surrounding Jesus, Peter proclaimed: "Him, being delivered by the determined purpose and foreknowledge of God, you have taken by lawless hands, have crucified, and put to death; whom God raised up, having loosed the pains of death, because it was not possible that He should be held by it" (Acts 2:23–24). We've already seen Paul citing the resurrection of Jesus in his discourse with the philosophers at Athens (Acts 17:31). Paul writes that he preached Christ crucified but also that His crucifixion was not the final word. Notice the varied references to the resurrection.

> For if when we were enemies we were reconciled to God through the death of His Son, much more, having been reconciled, we shall be saved by His life. (Rom. 5:10)

> For I delivered to you first of all that which I also received: that Christ died for our sins according to the Scriptures, and that He was buried, and that He rose again the third day according to the Scriptures. (1 Cor. 15:3–4)

> And without controversy great is the mystery of godliness:
> God was manifested in the flesh,
> Justified in the Spirit,
> Seen by angels,
> Preached among the Gentiles,
> Believed on in the world,
> Received up in glory. (1 Tim. 3:16)

The story of Christ's mission is one of conquest. He didn't leave us guessing. He conquered sin, death, and the grave—for those in bondage to them (see Eph. 2:6).

Two words never carried so much weight. Jesus *died* and *rose*. The credibility of Christianity and the legitimacy of the gospel depend on their veracity. Because of that import, we will devote attention to Christ's resurrection as we did to His crucifixion, looking at its fact, its necessity, and its promise.

The Verdict

I enjoy mystery novels. One of my favorite genres is the legal thriller that combines mystery with courtroom drama. In legal thrillers the verdict is based on evidence brought forth. That evidence needs to be unearthed and presented in such a way that the narrative makes sense and adequately accounts for all the facts.

We can take this approach to verifying Jesus's resurrection from the grave. In fact, that is the approach Peter takes in his sermon to the crowd gathered in Jerusalem for the feast of Pentecost following Christ's resurrection. People had traveled from all over for the occasion. They were abuzz with recent events that made that Pentecost like no other. In his sermon in Acts 2 Peter brings to bear four strands of evidence that lead to an inescapable conclusion.

The Man

Peter begins by pointing to Jesus, particularly as one distinguished by God: "Men of Israel, hear these words: Jesus of Nazareth, a Man attested by God to you by miracles, wonders, and signs which God did through Him in your midst, as you yourselves also know" (Acts 2:22). Peter highlights two things in particular. He identifies Him as Jesus *of Nazareth*. Jesus is His given name. Nazareth refers to His hometown, where He was raised. This is a common manner of identification in the Bible, narrowing it down from all those who bear a common name. For example, Saul is called Saul of Tarsus.

Sometimes people are identified by their lineage, such as Simon bar Jonah, Simon son of Jonah. But for reasons we've already touched on, identifying Jesus as the son of Joseph would be inappropriate. Associating Jesus with Nazareth makes Him a known quantity and gives Him roots just like anyone else would have, roots that have significance for prophetic anticipation and validation (see Matt. 2:23).

The second thing Peter highlights about Jesus distinguishes Him from everyone else, providing definitive identification. Peter could have referenced the proclamation from God that he had heard with James and John at the Mount of Transfiguration (Matt. 17:1–6), but that was private knowledge, not public. What was public were all the miracles, signs, and wonders Jesus did. Many in the multitude had seen personally or heard through the grapevine the stupendous acts of Jesus in healing the sick, giving sight to the blind, and even raising the dead. Peter explained these mighty acts as pointing not to the deity of Christ but to the "*Man* attested by God," the Man Jesus, with a known hometown, credentialed by God. It was as if Peter brought God Himself to the witness stand to authenticate Jesus as the Son of Man sent by God.

The Plan

In presenting a case, attorneys will construct a narrative that fits the facts of the case. A prosecuting attorney will frame an account that shows the defendant to be guilty. The defense attorney will take the same facts and paint a much different picture, one that exonerates his or her client. Peter constructs a narrative that aligns with the plan and purpose of God, putting the events surrounding the Man Jesus in biblical context: "Him, being delivered by the determined purpose and foreknowledge of God, you have taken by lawless hands, have crucified, and put to death; whom God raised up, having loosed the pains of death, because it was not possible that He should be held by it" (Acts 2:23–24).

Peter puts the events in the context of the plan of God, which we might think of as a metanarrative, or redemptive narrative. This bigger picture governs the events of the day and the actions of men, including the sinful actions of betraying an innocent man. The people were responsible and culpable for their actions, yet God's plan superintended and enfolded those actions.

We see a similar scene in the book of Genesis when Joseph addressed his brothers, who had sold him into slavery: "Do not be afraid, for am I in the place of God? But as for you, you meant evil against me; but God meant it for good, in order to bring it about as it is this day, to save many people alive" (Gen. 50:19–20). Joseph doesn't excuse the actions of his brothers in any sense, but he affirms that God ruled them for His purposes. Just as the story of Joseph, the narrative surrounding Jesus tells of redemption, in which the sinful actions of people serve the providential intentions of the sovereign God.

Expert Witnesses
Having identified Jesus and laid out the divine narrative of Jesus on a mission from God, Peter starts to bring witness testimony to bear. In a trial, sometimes witnesses will be called to the stand to relate what they personally saw. It sounds like Peter could have called any number of people to testify since he says of the people "as you yourselves also know" (Acts 2:22). That's what witnesses do. They tell what they directly

know. But the first witnesses that Peter appeals to are *expert* witnesses. An eyewitness to a car accident would testify to what he saw, such as one car running a red light and plowing into another. An expert witness might be brought in to present a forensic analysis of the accident scene describing tire skid marks, meaning of points of impact, and even surveillance camera data.

Sometimes the testimony of expert witnesses is colored by which side is paying them. The expert witnesses Peter brings to the fore, however, are those whose word is truth as spokesmen of God Himself. In this case Peter brings their testimony to bear not by bringing them to the front to address the crowd but by reading their depositions into the record.

Peter opened his address to the crowd with the expert witness of a prophet named Joel. Joel gives flavor to the remarkable events that had happened, including the related outpouring of the Holy Spirit. Here's the recorded statement Peter brings to bear:

> And it shall come to pass in the last days, says God,
> That I will pour out of My Spirit on all flesh;
> Your sons and your daughters shall prophesy,
> Your young men shall see visions,
> Your old men shall dream dreams.
> And on My menservants and on My maidservants
> I will pour out My Spirit in those days;
> And they shall prophesy.
> I will show wonders in heaven above
> And signs in the earth beneath:
> Blood and fire and vapor of smoke.
> The sun shall be turned into darkness,
> And the moon into blood,

Before the coming of the great and awesome day
    of the LORD.
And it shall come to pass
That whoever calls on the name of the LORD
Shall be saved. (Acts 2:17–21)

The expert testimony couches the events at Pentecost as the "last days," the final chapter of God's history of redemption that began in the book of Genesis. The theme of the story has to do with salvation.

Another expert witness that Peter lays before the people is David, a prophet like Joel as an instrument of God's speaking, but unlike Joel, a king over God's people. David was an actual king over ancient Israel, but he was also someone who represented the greater King to come, who would rule over a greater kingdom. Here is David's deposition about Jesus, quoting from Psalm 16:

For David says concerning Him:

"I foresaw the LORD always before my face,
For He is at my right hand, that I may not be shaken.
Therefore my heart rejoiced, and my tongue was glad;
Moreover my flesh also will rest in hope.
For You will not leave my soul in Hades,
Nor will You allow Your Holy One to see corruption.
You have made known to me the ways of life;
You will make me full of joy in Your presence."
(Acts 2:25–28)

After reading this deposition, Peter looks out at the crowd and explains that David's prophecy wasn't about himself but about Jesus:

Men and brethren, let me speak freely to you of the patriarch David, that he is both dead and buried, and his tomb is with us to this day. Therefore, being a prophet, and knowing that God had sworn with an oath to him that of the fruit of his body, according to the flesh, He would raise up the Christ to sit on his throne, he, foreseeing this, spoke concerning the resurrection of the Christ, that His soul was not left in Hades, nor did His flesh see corruption. (Acts 2:29–31)

By citing these expert witnesses, Peter expands the narrative to the whole of the Bible to explain to the crowd gathered for Pentecost the seismic nature of the events happening in their day.

Eyewitnesses

For his last strain of evidence, Peter turns to eyewitnesses. An eyewitness is one who personally experiences something and so can give direct evidence versus hearsay. "This Jesus God has raised up, of which we are all witnesses" (Acts 2:32).

The sheer number of witnesses to the risen Christ is overwhelming. Peter had himself seen the risen Christ. The other apostles had seen Jesus alive after His crucifixion. The apostle Paul gives us a witness list: "[Jesus] was seen by Cephas, then by the twelve. After that He was seen by over five hundred brethren at once, of whom the greater part remain to the present, but some have fallen asleep. After that He was seen by James, then by all the apostles. Then last of all He was seen by me also, as by one born out of due time" (1 Cor. 15:5–8).

Having presented irrefutable and insurmountable evidence, Peter pulls it all together with a closing argument:

Therefore being exalted to the right hand of God, and having received from the Father the promise of the Holy Spirit, He poured out this which you now see and hear.

For David did not ascend into the heavens, but he says himself:

"The LORD said to my Lord,
'Sit at My right hand,
Till I make Your enemies Your footstool.'"

Therefore let all the house of Israel know assuredly that God has made this Jesus, whom you crucified, both Lord and Christ. (Acts 2:33–36)

Twice, Peter uses the word "therefore," pressing an inescapable conclusion. Jesus is not dead but alive. He lives as the Christ of God.

The Value

The case built by Peter at Pentecost, the record of the four Gospels, and the testimony of the Epistles make clear that Jesus was raised from the dead. But what if He had not been? What difference would an occupied tomb make? Wouldn't Jesus still have had a profound impact on the world? For that matter, what difference does it make if Jesus has been raised from the dead?

How do we know that something actually works? I was in need of a new computer. The old one took so long to load that I would have been better off with ink and quill to capture my ideas before they dissipated into the irretrievable abyss of the forgotten. I spotted a deal that I couldn't refuse, so I took the plunge and placed the order. I received the new machine within the week and was all geared up to finally have a computer that worked. After unpacking and setting everything up, I turned it on. Nothing. I checked to make sure it was plugged in. It was. The light on the monitor glowed green, but the computer itself was a dud right from the box.

How do we know Jesus's accomplishment on the cross actually worked—that it was effective? Jesus came to atone for sin's guilt and free His people from sin's grip, but how do we know if He was successful? Paul gives us the answer and helps us to think through the ramifications of Christ's resurrection. He begins with the prospect for us if Jesus has *not* been raised from the dead:

> Now if Christ is preached that He has been raised from the dead, how do some among you say that there is no resurrection of the dead? But if there is no resurrection of the dead, then Christ is not risen. And if Christ is not risen, then our preaching is empty and your faith is also empty. Yes, and we are found false witnesses of God, because we have testified of God that He raised up Christ, whom He did not raise up—if in fact the dead do not rise. For if the dead do not rise, then Christ is not risen. And if Christ is not risen, your faith is futile; you are still in your sins! Then also those who have fallen asleep in Christ have perished. If in this life only we have hope in Christ, we are of all men the most pitiable. (1 Cor. 15:12–19)

A full tomb means a futile faith. As we saw in chapter 1, faith is not in faith. Faith is founded on fact. If Christ's resurrection is not a fact, our faith is groundless. Jesus's work on the cross did not work. We open the box of the gospel to find it without power, no ability to save. We have believed a lie. We have lied to others. We are to be pitied like those who have invested in a scam.

But Paul doesn't leave us in such a miserable state. He quickly goes on to say: "But now Christ is risen from the dead, and has become the firstfruits of those who have fallen

asleep" (1 Cor. 15:20). All those horrors that Paul listed if
Jesus hasn't been raised are turned on their head. Christ is
risen. The hope of the gospel is real and extends into the age
to come. Death is conquered. The bondage of sin has been
broken. If our trust is in Christ for these things, then our
trust is founded. Our belief in the resurrection of the body
that we assert later in the third section of the Apostles' Creed
is legitimate. We'll explore what it means for us to be part of
the harvest of which Jesus is the firstfruits when we get to
that section, but suffice it to say now that the cupboard of
hope is not bare.

We who have hoped in Christ receive every blessing
bound up in Him because He lives. John records what this
means for those who trust in Him: "I am He who lives, and
was dead, and behold, I am alive forevermore. Amen. And I
have the keys of Hades and of Death" (Rev. 1:18). Not only
is the green light of power lit, the success of Christ operates
as promised.

The Creed expresses this reality of hope by saying that
Jesus "rose again from the dead." While that is a true statement, one used elsewhere for Christ's resurrection (e.g., Acts
10:41; 1 Thess. 4:14), it might be more helpful to understand
Jesus as *being raised* (e.g., Acts 3:15; Rom. 6:4, 9), again looking to Jesus in His true and full humanity. Just as we will be
raised from the dead, Jesus as man, as our representative in
humanity, was raised from the dead by God (Acts 3:15; Rom.
8:11) in declaration of the satisfaction of His justice and in
vindication of His saving work. In fact, Paul puts it in a way
that is strange to our ears. He speaks of Jesus "who was delivered up because of our offenses, and was raised because of our
justification" (Rom. 4:25). So much are we as the redeemed of

the Lord identified with Jesus in His crucifixion and resurrection that Paul says this:

> And without controversy great is the mystery of godliness:
> > God was manifested in the flesh,
> > Justified in the Spirit,
> > Seen by angels,
> > Preached among the Gentiles,
> > Believed on in the world,
> > Received up in glory. (1 Tim. 3:16)

Jesus's justification is our justification. His vindication in respect to the requirements of God's law is our vindication. His resurrection secures and anticipates our resurrection.

Reign and Return of the Risen One

Jesus rose bodily from the grave, but where is He now and what is He doing? Jesus came into this world in the humblest of ways—born a helpless baby in an obscure town among the animals in a stable. He was born a king but yet to conquer. Christ left the world, however, in glory, having accomplished His saving mission, all authority on heaven and earth being given to Him. Luke describes His departure from earth's soil:

> Therefore, when they had come together, they asked Him, saying, "Lord, will You at this time restore the kingdom to Israel?" And He said to them, "It is not for you to know times or seasons which the Father has put in His own authority. But you shall receive power when the Holy Spirit has come upon you; and you shall be witnesses to Me in Jerusalem, and in all Judea and Samaria, and to the end of the earth."

> Now when He had spoken these things, while they watched, He was taken up, and a cloud received Him out of their sight. And while they looked steadfastly toward heaven as He went up, behold, two men stood by them in white apparel, who also said, "Men of Galilee, why do you stand gazing up into heaven? This same Jesus, who was taken up from you into heaven, will so come in like manner as you saw Him go into heaven." (Acts 1:6–11)

Two things stand out to us. One, the work of Christ continues to build His kingdom. Two, there will come a day when that work will be completed and Jesus will return.

Jesus may be bodily absent from this world, but that does not mean He is not with us. At the close of Matthew's gospel, where Jesus issues the command to go into all the world to make disciples, He assures His ambassadors then as He does now that He is with us, to the very end of the age (see 28:19–20). The "age" speaks to the day of salvation, this time while the gospel continues to go forth by the witness of His followers, until the age to come is ushered in.

When Jesus was with His disciples in the upper room, He says something both comforting and emboldening:

> If you love Me, keep My commandments. And I will pray the Father, and He will give you another Helper, that He may abide with you forever—the Spirit of truth, whom the world cannot receive, because it neither sees Him nor knows Him; but you know Him, for He dwells with you and will be in you. I will not leave you orphans; I will come to you.
>
> A little while longer and the world will see Me no more, but you will see Me. Because I live, you will live

also. At that day you will know that I am in My Father, and you in Me, and I in you. (John 14:15–20)

So even though Jesus is not physically present with us, He is with us by the Holy Spirit sent after the resurrection. He is with us to comfort and encourage us, and He is with us for the work of building His church. What a blessed assurance for our personal salvation and for the confidence that Jesus is the one gathering His sheep and so building His church!

This realization of the risen Christ reigning on high for His church is a subject of prayer for our increasing realization, confidence, and courage in our work as witnesses:

Therefore I also, after I heard of your faith in the Lord Jesus and your love for all the saints, do not cease to give thanks for you, making mention of you in my prayers: that the God of our Lord Jesus Christ, the Father of glory, may give to you the spirit of wisdom and revelation in the knowledge of Him, the eyes of your understanding being enlightened; that you may know what is the hope of His calling, what are the riches of the glory of His inheritance in the saints, and what is the exceeding greatness of His power toward us who believe, according to the working of His mighty power which He worked in Christ when He raised Him from the dead and seated Him at His right hand in the heavenly places, far above all principality and power and might and dominion, and every name that is named, not only in this age but also in that which is to come.

And He put all things under His feet, and gave Him to be head over all things to the church, which is His body, the fullness of Him who fills all in all. (Eph. 1:15–23)

Jesus's reign is not like that of some king whose kingdom covers a vast amount of territory and whose subjects know of him by reputation. The kingdom of Christ fills all in all, and by the Spirit Jesus is personally present wherever His kingdom extends, exhibited in the hearts of those who have bowed the knee before Him.

One of the ways Christ's reign on high is described is through His intercession. That's another way of saying that Jesus represents those for whom He died (see Col. 3:1–4). In contrasting the provisional priests of the Old Testament with Jesus as the perfect Priest who has perpetual priesthood, the writer of Hebrews speaks to the intercession of Jesus: "Also there were many priests, because they were prevented by death from continuing. But He, because He continues forever, has an unchangeable priesthood. Therefore He is also able to save to the uttermost those who come to God through Him, since He always lives to make intercession for them" (7:23–25).

Imagine being in debt to the IRS. You've found protection through an attorney who advocates for you. When in the presence of the IRS agent you find boldness and comfort with your attorney beside you. But when that attorney steps out of the room even for a moment, leaving you alone with the agent, you squirm and fret. This crude illustration gives us a sense of the comfort and confidence that are ours knowing Jesus is always in the presence of the Father representing us by virtue of His atoning work on the cross and vindicating resurrection from the dead. Paul expresses this glorious truth in the context of God's glorious grace:

> What then shall we say to these things? If God is for us, who can be against us? He who did not spare His own Son, but delivered Him up for us all, how shall He not with Him also freely give us all things? Who shall

bring a charge against God's elect? It is God who justifies. Who is he who condemns? It is Christ who died,
and furthermore is also risen, who is even at the right
hand of God, who also makes intercession for us. (Rom.
8:31–34)

The "right hand" refers to the position of preeminence and
privilege bestowed upon Jesus as our representative, who
died for us and now lives for us.

The Bible's teaching about Jesus's reign is often coupled
with reference to His return, something the angel indicated at
Jesus's ascension. In the book of Revelation, the movement of
history presses on, like waves lapping on the shore advancing
the incoming tide, toward the return of Christ. We live now
awaiting, anticipating, longing for that return. The first chapter sets the tone:

John, to the seven churches which are in Asia:
Grace to you and peace from Him who is and who
was and who is to come, and from the seven Spirits
who are before His throne, and from Jesus Christ, the
faithful witness, the firstborn from the dead, and the
ruler over the kings of the earth.

To Him who loved us and washed us from our sins
in His own blood, and has made us kings and priests
to His God and Father, to Him be glory and dominion
forever and ever. Amen.

Behold, He is coming with clouds, and every eye will
see Him, even they who pierced Him. And all the tribes
of the earth will mourn because of Him. Even so, Amen.

"I am the Alpha and the Omega, the Beginning and
the End," says the Lord, "who is and who was and who
is to come, the Almighty." (vv. 4–8)

Right now Christ is building His church. His kingdom is growing to fill the earth. But one day, Jesus will return to usher in His kingdom in fullness. His second coming will not be in humility to shed His blood but in exaltation to claim those for whom He died. In His first coming Jesus did not come to judge or condemn (John 3:17–18; 12:47). In His return it will be a different matter (John 5:24–27; Acts 17:31; 2 Tim. 4:1; Heb. 9:27).

The sacrament of the Lord's Supper reminds us of the return of Christ every time we celebrate it. We remember the Lord's death *until He comes*. We lift up the cup of blessing (1 Cor. 10:16) because Jesus was lifted up to take from our hand the cup of wrath (Ps. 75:8; Luke 22:42). Our communion is with the risen Lord as a people bonded in His blood, awaiting the day when faith will be sight and we will be with our Lord in glory forever.

We saw in Jesus's burial that a stone was rolled over the mouth of the cave. The stone was quite large and heavy. In fact, on that resurrection morn the women who carried spices to the tomb to anoint the body of Jesus asked themselves: "'Who will roll away the stone from the door of the tomb for us?' But when they looked up, they saw that the stone had been rolled away—for it was very large" (Mark 16:3–4).

The reason the stone was rolled away was not so Jesus could get out. Jesus's resurrection body was physical, but it was also glorified, able to pass through walls (see John 20:19–29). The stone was moved not to allow Jesus exit but to allow others entrance. The women first, and later Peter and John, saw for themselves that the occupied grave was now empty, save for the grave linen. Jesus had been raised, as He said.

The record of God's Word, the trial transcript of Peter's sermon at Pentecost, serves as that rolled-away stone, allowing us to look inside, calling us to rest in this Savior by faith, that His return in judgment will be for us a day of joy and gladness, not dread and doom. After presenting his evidence in Acts 2 confirming that Jesus is both Lord and Christ, we find this response from those who heard:

> Now when they heard this, they were cut to the heart, and said to Peter and the rest of the apostles, "Men and brethren, what shall we do?"
>
> Then Peter said to them, "Repent, and let every one of you be baptized in the name of Jesus Christ for the remission of sins; and you shall receive the gift of the Holy Spirit. For the promise is to you and to your children, and to all who are afar off, as many as the Lord our God will call." (Acts 2:37–39)

Every time it is recited, the Apostles' Creed presses the question of where we stand in respect to Jesus.

7

THE HOLY SPIRIT

I believe in the Holy Spirit.

In reciting the Apostles' Creed, what do we mean when we declare that we believe in the Holy Spirit? We have already stated that the Creed is an expression of the Christian faith. If that is the case, then it is no surprise to find the Holy Spirit as a headliner along with the Father and the Son. Christianity holds to a God who is triune—one God in three persons.

Like the Apostles' Creed, the Nicene Creed mentions Father, Son, and Holy Spirit. But while the Apostles' Creed does not expand on the person of the Holy Spirit, the Nicene Creed says this: "And I believe in the Holy Spirit, the Lord and giver of life, who proceeds from the Father and the Son; who with the Father and the Son together is worshipped and glorified."

The curious thing is what the Apostles' Creed does not say. That nothing is said in the Apostles' Creed to describe the Holy Spirit suggests that the creeds had different purposes. While the Apostles' Creed was written *to summarize* the Christian faith, the Nicene Creed was composed *to defend* the Christian faith. The Nicene Creed arose as a statement of the church from councils convened to combat heresy. Attacks had risen from within the Christian community against the deity and unity of the person of Jesus Christ and the deity and origin of the Holy Spirit. Through its councils, the church responded to these attacks by issuing a detailed defense. That defense can be seen in the careful wording used to describe Jesus and the Holy Spirit. So while the Apostles' Creed affirms the Trinity, the Nicene Creed defends the Bible's teaching about God in three persons.

How then does the Apostles' Creed present the Holy Spirit?

> I believe in the Holy Spirit,
> the holy catholic church,
> the communion of saints,
> the forgiveness of sins,
> the resurrection of the body,
> and the life everlasting.

At first the list seems rather random, as though the third section of the Creed were a miscellaneous category, a catchall for Christian belief, and certainly off topic from believing in the Holy Spirit—until we realize that the Apostles' Creed instructs us not just in the Trinity but in the Trinitarian character of salvation. What is given us in the third section of the Creed is not a character description but a job description. The Spirit is being cast not in His eternal being but in His redemptive doing. We could put it this way:

- I believe in the Holy Spirit, who forms, unifies, and empowers the church.

- I believe in the fellowship of the Holy Spirit among God's saints.

- I believe in the Holy Spirit, who works faith and confers forgiveness of sins.

- I believe in the Holy Spirit, who raises the dead.

- I believe in the Holy Spirit, who bestows eternal life.

Like an epistle that transitions from theological ground-work to applied theology, the Apostles' Creed moves from the accomplished work of Jesus Christ to the application of that work by the Holy Spirit. For example, Paul's letter to the Ephesians moves from the calling of God in salvation from the foundation of the world and the work of His Son to the outworking of that calling in the trenches of everyday life. The letter divides after chapter 3 with these words: "I, there-fore, the prisoner of the Lord, beseech you to walk worthy of the calling with which you were called" (4:1).

From that note Paul unpacks how to go about living in newness of life for the glory of God as individuals, spouses, parents, and workers in society and in the church. Prominent in this practical living is the presence and power of the Holy Spirit (3:16; 4:3–4; 5:9; 6:17–18). Even where the Spirit is not explicitly referenced, He is present throughout in bringing Christ to us for the Christian life and the functioning of the church. When the gathered church recites the Creed, it pro-claims its source of life and power through the Holy Spirit.

Were it asked, the Apostles' Creed would affirm the same thing about the Holy Spirit that the Nicene Creed affirms. But the former was given a different task—laying out as a matter of faith how the salvation achieved by Jesus Christ comes to believers and transforms their lives. How does the work of Jesus laid out in section 2 of the Creed work out in section 3 in bringing the blessings of salvation to us? Let's begin with the template of Trinitarian triumph that opens Paul's letter to the Ephesians:

> Blessed be the God and Father of our Lord Jesus Christ, who has blessed us with every spiritual blessing in the heavenly places in Christ, just as He chose us in Him before the foundation of the world, that we should be holy and without blame before Him in love, having predestined us to adoption as sons by Jesus Christ to Himself, according to the good pleasure of His will, to the praise of the glory of His grace, by which He made us accepted in the Beloved.
>
> In Him we have redemption through His blood, the forgiveness of sins, according to the riches of His grace which He made to abound toward us in all wisdom and prudence, having made known to us the mystery of His will, according to His good pleasure which He purposed in Himself, that in the dispensation of the fullness of the times He might gather together in one all things in Christ, both which are in heaven and which are on earth—in Him. In Him also we have obtained an inheritance, being predestined according to the purpose of Him who works all things according to the counsel of His will, that we who first trusted in Christ should be to the praise of His glory.
>
> In Him you also trusted, after you heard the word of truth, the gospel of your salvation; in whom also, having believed, you were sealed with the Holy Spirit of promise, who is the guarantee of our inheritance until the redemption of the purchased possession, to the praise of His glory. (1:3–14)

These twelve verses are one sentence in the original language of the New Testament. It is almost as if they are to be said in one breath, one exhalation of praise. The purposes of God the Father, achieved in Christ the Son, find their goal in us through the Holy Spirit. But how?

Spirit of Christ

The Holy Spirit is God, the third member of the Trinity. He has always existed, uncreated along with the Father and the Son. We see the distinct members of the Trinity identified in Scripture. For example, in the Great Commission Jesus speaks of baptism in the *name* of the Father and of the Son and of the Holy Spirit, demonstrating that there is one God (Matt. 28:19). Paul's benediction to close his second letter to the church at Corinth references the members of the God-head: "The grace of the Lord Jesus Christ, and the love of God, and the communion of the Holy Spirit be with you all. Amen" (13:14).

There is one God (one name) but three distinct persons. But when we turn to the New Testament, we might be surprised to find that the lines of distinction seem to be blurred. In some places Paul speaks of the Spirit of God (Rom. 15:19; 1 Cor. 6:11). In other places he speaks of the Spirit of Christ (Phil. 1:19), as does Peter (1 Peter 1:11). In one sense, since there is one God, we can ascribe the character and movements of God to all the members of the Trinity. For example, Jesus is the head of His church and the one who shed His blood for the church. But we read this: "Therefore take heed to yourselves and to all the flock, among which the Holy Spirit has made you overseers, to shepherd the church of God which He purchased with His own blood" (Acts 20:28).

As we've seen, though, often the members of the Trinity are portrayed in the New Testament in their respective roles of salvation, as we saw in the passage from Ephesians 1. The Spirit is the one Jesus sent on completion of His saving work. Jesus explains this in His time with the disciples before His betrayal and crucifixion:

> And I will pray the Father, and He will give you another Helper, that He may abide with you forever—the Spirit of truth, whom the world cannot receive, because it neither sees Him nor knows Him; but you know Him, for He dwells with you and will be in you. I will not leave you orphans; I will come to you. (John 14:16–18)

> But when the Helper comes, whom I shall send to you from the Father, the Spirit of truth who proceeds from the Father, He will testify of Me. (John 15:26)

> Nevertheless I tell you the truth. It is to your advantage that I go away; for if I do not go away, the Helper will not come to you; but if I depart, I will send Him to you. (John 16:7)

Jesus would come to us by His Spirit. The blessings of the Father, achieved by the Son, would be dispensed through the Spirit. Not the Spirit in Himself, but the Spirit who brings Christ to us so that we would no longer be orphans but instead children of the living God. As Paul puts it to the Galatians: "And because you are sons, God has sent forth the Spirit of His Son into your hearts, crying out, 'Abba, Father!'" (4:6). To speak of the Spirit of Christ is not to point to the nonphysical aspect of Jesus's humanity (body and spirit) but to speak of the Holy Spirit sent by God through whom Christ comes to us.

We discover how that works by looking at the role of the Holy Spirit in respect to Jesus as the Anointed One of God:[1]

- Jesus was conceived by the Holy Spirit in the womb of the virgin Mary (Luke 1:35).

- Jesus was baptized by the Holy Spirit at the outset of His public ministry (Luke 3:21–22).

- Jesus, as the second Adam representing His sheep, was led by the Spirit into the wilderness to do battle with Satan (Luke 4:1).

- The Spirit rested upon Jesus throughout His earthly life and public ministry to preach the good news, to proclaim liberty to the captives, and to provide ransom (Luke 4:18).

- Jesus was raised from the dead by the Holy Spirit (Rom. 8:11).

The Spirit was upon Jesus in all that He did in His obedience and sacrifice. It was this Spirit, the Spirit of the risen Christ, who was sent to apply the work of Christ to those given Him by the Father. The Spirit takes what is Christ's and makes it ours.

Paul makes this connection between the saving work of Christ and His blessings conferred upon us. In speaking of the benefit of justification, which includes the forgiveness of sins mentioned by the Creed, the apostle says this: "Who shall bring a charge against God's elect? It is God who justifies. Who is he who condemns? It is Christ who died, and

---

1. *Messiah* (Hebrew) and *Christ* (Greek) mean "Anointed One."

furthermore is also risen, who is even at the right hand of God, who also makes intercession for us" (Rom. 8:33–34). Our forgiveness is gained in Christ's death, resurrection, and reign. Paul attributes that connection to the Holy Spirit:

> But you are not in the flesh but in the Spirit, if indeed the Spirit of God dwells in you. Now if anyone does not have the Spirit of Christ, he is not His. And if Christ is in you, the body is dead because of sin, but the Spirit is life because of righteousness. But if the Spirit of Him who raised Jesus from the dead dwells in you, He who raised Christ from the dead will also give life to your mortal bodies through His Spirit who dwells in you. (Rom. 8:9–11)

The Spirit brings Christ to us, uniting us to Him in His saving work. The Spirit of God who dwells in us is the Spirit of Christ who raised Jesus from the dead.

Some lament that the church today does not focus enough on the Holy Spirit. He is called the forgotten member of the Trinity. But Jesus Himself pointed out that the role of the Spirit was to testify to Jesus and bring glory to Him:

> However, when He, the Spirit of truth, has come, He will guide you into all truth; for He will not speak on His own authority, but whatever He hears He will speak; and He will tell you things to come. He will glorify Me, for He will take of what is Mine and declare it to you. All things that the Father has are Mine. Therefore I said that He will take of Mine and declare it to you. (John 16:13–15)

The Spirit does not work independently in salvation, but in respect to Christ. Paul emphasized that his message was Jesus Christ and Him crucified. He summarizes the gospel by focusing on the work of Christ on the cross as central. On one side of the cross is the life of Christ. On the other side is the *new* life of Christ. When Paul speaks of this message finding its home in the hearts of sinners, he points us to the Holy Spirit:

> And I, brethren, when I came to you, did not come with excellence of speech or of wisdom declaring to you the testimony of God. For I determined not to know anything among you except Jesus Christ and Him crucified. I was with you in weakness, in fear, and in much trembling. And my speech and my preaching were not with persuasive words of human wisdom, but in demonstration of the Spirit and of power, that your faith should not be in the wisdom of men but in the power of God. (1 Cor. 2:1–5)

God alone—Father, Son, and Holy Spirit—is the author of salvation, from its purpose in eternity to its purchase in history, to its pursuit of us in our personal experience.

The Blessings of the Holy Spirit

Ephesians tells us that God has blessed us with every spiritual blessing in the heavenlies in Christ Jesus. This cornucopia of blessing becomes ours through the Holy Spirit. The blessings of the Spirit are the blessings of Christ conferred to us. As the final section of the Apostles' Creed suggests, these blessings are poured out by the Spirit at both an individual level and a community level—the Christian and the church.

Individual Blessing

I came to faith in Christ as an adult, a twenty-year-old college senior. Growing up with some religious influence, I heard the stories of the Bible. I knew Jesus was born in a stable, had died on a cross, and had risen from the dead. They were simply particulars of the religious tradition in which I was raised. In college, I rejected this brand of religion not so much as untrue but as irrelevant. I could live life just fine without it. Every once in a while Christians would engage me in conversation about Jesus. I regarded them as naïve and unintellectual and rejected their message. When I approached my senior year, something began to happen. As I listened to this teaching, it started to make sense to me. It became meaningful. Eventually, it became necessary. By grace, that's when I took the step of committing my life to Jesus Christ as my Savior and Lord.

What happened? How did the same old, same old suddenly start to find appeal for me? The information wasn't new. The answer is the Holy Spirit. He gave me ears to hear and a heart to embrace this unique and amazing Savior. By the Spirit's direct operation in my heart, I shared the simple testimony of the blind man in John 9: "One thing I know: that though I was blind, now I see" (v. 25). The Spirit brought to me what He brings to every Christian.

New birth. The Bible describes every person born as dead in sin (Eph. 2:1; Col. 2:13). They are physically alive but spiritually dead—dead men walking. How can a dead man turn to Christ? He cannot (Rom. 8:8). He first needs spiritual life. That life comes from the Holy Spirit. Jesus explained that to a religious teacher of His day in terms of being born again: "Most assuredly, I say to you, unless one is born again, he cannot see the kingdom of God.... Most assuredly, I say to you, unless one is born of water and the Spirit, he cannot enter the kingdom of God. That which is born of the flesh is flesh, and that which is born of the Spirit is spirit" (John 3:3, 5–6).

Every Christian has the backstory of being dead in sin and, by God's grace, being made alive in Jesus Christ (Eph. 2:1–9).[2] Through that new life the unresponsive become responsive; the hardened become receptive to the things of God. The apostle Paul lays out the birth certificate of the believer in triune glory:

> But when the kindness and the love of God our Savior toward man appeared, not by works of righteousness which we have done, but according to His mercy He saved us, through the washing of regeneration and renewing of the Holy Spirit, whom He poured out on us abundantly through Jesus Christ our Savior, that having been justified by His grace we should become heirs according to the hope of eternal life. (Titus 3:4–7)

The word "regeneration" is the one that speaks to the new birth, born again of the Holy Spirit. I can well identify with the apostle's explanation of why the things that were so distasteful to me began to become savory with the seasoning of grace and urgent for me: "But the natural man does not receive the things of the Spirit of God, for they are foolishness to him; nor can he know them, because they are spiritually discerned" (1 Cor. 2:14). Those things of Jesus that were silly to me became words of life, all by the work of the Holy Spirit to change me.

---

2. For direction in the theology and example of a personal testimony, see Stanley D. Gale, *Community Houses of Prayer Ministry Manual* (Los Alamos, N.M.: Deo Volente Publishing, 2007), 211–16.

New life. With new birth comes new life and new status. The Holy Spirit who gives us life in Christ grows us in Christ. Just like a baby grows physically and matures, so does a Christian. That growth is by the Holy Spirit.

In Christ, we have a new identity as children of God, along with all the rights, privileges, and expectations that brings. Adoption is the richest of all God's blessings (Rom. 8:14–17). John can barely contain himself in speaking about it: "Behold what manner of love the Father has bestowed on us, that we should be called children of God!" (1 John 3:1). John marvels at the extent of the love of God in adopting those who were His enemies. Paul explains how the blessing of adoption (Eph. 1:5) in Christ comes to us:

> But when the fullness of the time had come, God sent forth His Son, born of a woman, born under the law, to redeem those who were under the law, that we might receive the adoption as sons.
>
> And because you are sons, God has sent forth the Spirit of His Son into your hearts, crying out, "Abba, Father!" Therefore you are no longer a slave but a son, and if a son, then an heir of God through Christ. (Gal. 4:4–7)

"Abba" is a term of endearment and intimacy. Because of the Holy Spirit, we are able to call God our Father. The Spirit bears witness to us of that glorious fact and helps us in our fellowship with the Father (Rom. 8:16, 26).

Part of this new life in Christ is a new standing. We were enemies of God, the sentence of condemnation hanging over our heads. But God justified us. We saw that term in Titus 3:4–5. In the book of Romans, Paul makes it clear that all humanity is on equal footing—sinners guilty before the judgment seat of God and under the sentence of just condemnation. He frames Jesus's work in respect to this predicament, first saying we cannot *make up* for sins we commit or *measure up* to the standard of perfect obedience demanded by the law of God:

> Now we know that whatever the law says, it says to those who are under the law, that every mouth may be stopped, and all the world may become guilty before God. Therefore by the deeds of the law no flesh will be justified in His sight, for by the law is the knowledge of sin.
>
> But now the righteousness of God apart from the law is revealed, being witnessed by the Law and the Prophets, even the righteousness of God, through faith in Jesus Christ, to all and on all who believe. For there is no difference; for all have sinned and fall short of the glory of God, being justified freely by His grace through the redemption that is in Christ Jesus, whom God set forth as a propitiation by His blood, through faith, to demonstrate His righteousness, because in His forbearance God had passed over the sins that were previously committed, to demonstrate at the present time His righteousness, that He might be just and the justifier of the one who has faith in Jesus. (Rom. 3:19–26)

The riddle of how God liberates sinners from the sentence of condemnation while remaining true to His holy character is solved in Jesus. He satisfied the debt of our sin. His spotless record of obedience is credited to us. That's justification. It involves both cleansing from sin's guilt and clothing with Christ's righteousness. It is this transaction of grace that the Spirit brings to us. It is justification that is in view when the Creed speaks of forgiveness of sin.

Finally, as part of our new life, the Spirit grows us in the image of Jesus (Gal. 4:19) and enables us to live in the power of Christ's resurrection. Paul prays that we would grow to know this power in increasing measure through the work of the Holy Spirit:

> For this reason I bow my knees to the Father of our Lord Jesus Christ, from whom the whole family in heaven and earth is named, that He would grant you, according to the riches of His glory, to be strengthened with might through His Spirit in the inner man, that Christ may dwell in your hearts through faith; that you, being rooted and grounded in love, may be able to comprehend with all the saints what is the width and length and depth and height—to know the love of Christ which passes knowledge; that you may be filled with all the fullness of God. (Eph. 3:14–19)

The Holy Spirit enables us to die to sin and live for Christ, as fruit of a transformed life: "But the fruit of the Spirit is love, joy, peace, longsuffering, kindness, goodness, faithfulness, gentleness, self-control. Against such there is no law. And those who are Christ's have crucified the flesh with its passions and desires. If we live in the Spirit, let us also walk in the Spirit" (Gal. 5:22–25).[3]

New hope. In the magisterial sentence of Ephesians 1:3–14, we are informed that the Holy Spirit is a seal to us: "In Him you also trusted, after you heard the word of truth, the gospel of your salvation; in whom also, having believed, you were

---

3. For more on this topic see Stanley D. Gale, *A Vine-Ripened Life: Spiritual Fruitfulness through Abiding in Christ* (Grand Rapids: Reformation Heritage Books, 2014).

sealed with the Holy Spirit of promise, who is the guarantee of our inheritance until the redemption of the purchased possession, to the praise of His glory" (vv. 13–14). The Spirit is called the Spirit of promise and a guarantee that reaches from here to eternity (2 Cor. 5:1–5). What that says is that nothing can separate us from the love of God for us in Jesus. The Spirit makes sure. What God began in us, He will see to completion. Every true believer will persevere to the end because he or she is preserved by the Spirit of promise. We live as pilgrims in this world in light of a future home with God. "For we through the Spirit eagerly wait for the hope of righteousness by faith" (Gal. 5:5).

The apostle Peter describes this inheritance for God's adopted children to those who are homeless and persecuted in this world:

> Blessed be the God and Father of our Lord Jesus Christ, who according to His abundant mercy has begotten us again to a living hope through the resurrection of Jesus Christ from the dead, to an inheritance incorruptible and undefiled and that does not fade away, reserved in heaven for you, who are kept by the power of God through faith for salvation ready to be revealed in the last time. (1 Peter 1:3–5)

This hope is rooted in Christ and guaranteed by the Spirit. Notice that our inheritance is held undiminished for us, and we are held for our inheritance by the power of God. That surety gives peace and joy in the pilgrimage to everyone whose trust is in Christ: "Now may the God of hope fill you with all joy and peace in believing, that you may abound in hope by the power of the Holy Spirit" (Rom. 15:13).

Community Blessings

The Spirit works not only in the individual; He works in the church, Christ's community of believers. In fact, the first areas noted in the Apostles' Creed in the section on the Holy Spirit relate to the church and the fellowship of believers with one another in the Spirit. The apostle Paul describes the unity of the Spirit in Ephesians 2:18–21:

> For through [Christ] we both have access by one Spirit to the Father.
>
> Now, therefore, you are no longer strangers and foreigners, but fellow citizens with the saints and members of the household of God, having been built on the foundation of the apostles and prophets, Jesus Christ Himself being the chief cornerstone, in whom the whole building, being fitted together, grows into a holy temple in the Lord.

We are called to maintain the unity of the Spirit with one another in the family of God (4:1–6).

Community is where we see unity in diversity. The Spirit of God is the headliner in Paul's discussion of spiritual gifts at work in the church:

> There are diversities of gifts, but the same Spirit. There are differences of ministries, but the same Lord. And there are diversities of activities, but it is the same God who works all in all. But the manifestation of the Spirit is given to each one for the profit of all: for to one is given the word of wisdom through the Spirit, to another the word of knowledge through the same Spirit, to another faith by the same Spirit, to another gifts of healings by the same Spirit, to another the working of miracles, to another prophecy, to another discerning of spirits, to another different kinds of tongues, to another the

> interpretation of tongues. But one and the same Spirit works all these things, distributing to each one individually as He wills. (1 Cor. 12:4–11)

Like a jigsaw puzzle with many irregular pieces, diversely gifted believers contribute to the picture of one body that functions for Jesus Christ (1 Cor. 12:14–20). Such gifts are not intended for personal aggrandizement but for community aggregation to the glory of God and blessing of one another.

Clearly, the Spirit is at work gathering, growing, and gifting Christ's church from its earliest stages to this day. The gifting of the church is attributed to the work of the Spirit. The Spirit brings individuals to embrace Christ (1 Cor. 12:3) and enfolds them into the body of Christ, His church (1 Cor. 12:12–13). The Spirit animates Christ's church with new life in Christ and inhabits the praise and work of the church for the sake of Christ's kingdom.

Believing in the Holy Spirit points us not only to the third member of the Trinity but also causes us to recognize the outworking of the accomplishments of Jesus Christ for His church, both individually and as a community.

8

THE CHURCH

I believe in... the holy catholic church,
the communion of saints.

When we think of the benefits of salvation, our minds tend to go to individual benefits like forgiveness of sin and eternal life. Certainly these are reasons for rejoicing. But in citing the Spirit's application of the work of Jesus Christ, the Apostles' Creed begins not with the individual but with the community. The "I believe" of the Creed is a belief shared with others for whom Christ died and lives. As we saw in the Great Commission at the close of Matthew's gospel, those who bow the knee in repentance and faith before the risen Lord Jesus are to be baptized and taught to obey. Baptism speaks to inclusion in the community of God's people, where they will be taught, encouraged in the faith, and cared for. They will be equipped and mobilized for the spread of the kingdom and building up of the church.

The Creed speaks of the church under two headings: holy and catholic, and communion of saints. Each of these descriptions offers a different perspective on the wonder of

God's redeeming love, the scope of Christ's saving work, and the bond of the Holy Spirit.

Holy

What does it mean for the church to be holy? Holiness can refer to a couple of different things. It can speak to moral purity. The Bible is full of teaching on the distinctive character of those in relationship with God in contrast to those who do not know God. The apostle Peter addresses the conduct of believers. He calls them aliens and sojourners, meaning that they were uprooted from their homeland. But it also suggests spiritual pilgrimage. Christians are *in* the world but not *of* the world. It's as if we were travelers in a foreign land, carrying the passport of heaven. The land, though, is foreign not only in the sense of being another country but especially in being foreign to the values, ethics, and priorities of those who are citizens of Christ's kingdom.

We find a wonderful example of this in the person of Daniel. Daniel and others of God's people were taken captive from Judah by an invading army in 605 BC and settled in the land of Babylon. Babylonian culture held to false gods. Daniel found himself in a society that did not believe in the true God and exerted an influence that tried to draw him away from God. Yet Daniel's heart was with God. The book of Daniel gives many accounts of this challenge for the Jews of being faithful to God and suffering because of it, even at the peril of their lives. Yet while Daniel was hated by some for his faith, he was esteemed by others, and so had an influence for the true God and made a contribution to the good of the society in which he found himself. Daniel was in the world, with all the trials and temptations that brings, yet he was not of the world, keeping his heart and ambition with God.

This world is not our home. We are to be light in darkness. One of the ways we distinguish ourselves is by living with a point of reference and a code of conduct that honor Jesus Christ. Peter describes the challenge for us, reminiscent of the same struggle Daniel faced: "Beloved, I beg you as sojourners and pilgrims, abstain from fleshly lusts which war against the soul, having your conduct honorable among the Gentiles, that when they speak against you as evildoers, they may, by your good works which they observe, glorify God in the day of visitation" (1 Peter 2:11–12). Since we are now children of God, adopted through the work of Jesus, we are to be holy, different from those who are not children of God: "As obedient children, not conforming yourselves to the former lusts, as in your ignorance; but as He who called you is holy, you also be holy in all your conduct, because it is written, 'Be holy, for I am holy'" (1 Peter 1:14–16).

Holiness has to do with consecration to God, where our lives flow out in reverence for Him and love for Jesus Christ in the power of the Holy Spirit. Paul summarizes a section on our distinctiveness from the world with these words: "Therefore, having these promises, beloved, let us cleanse ourselves from all filthiness of the flesh and spirit, perfecting holiness in the fear of God" (2 Cor. 7:1). Both Peter and Paul address us as "beloved." That term of endearment separates us as those on whom God has set His love, those Christ loved and died for. Holiness does not make us loved by God. Rather, holiness in conduct reflects our new identity in Christ as those loved. Paul describes this new identity and how it works out in holiness:

Therefore be imitators of God as dear children. And walk in love, as Christ also has loved us and given Himself for us, an offering and a sacrifice to God for a sweet-smelling aroma.

But fornication and all uncleanness or covetousness, let it not even be named among you, as is fitting for saints; neither filthiness, nor foolish talking, nor coarse jesting, which are not fitting, but rather giving of thanks. For this you know, that no fornicator, unclean person, nor covetous man, who is an idolater, has any inheritance in the kingdom of Christ and God. Let no one deceive you with empty words, for because of these things the wrath of God comes upon the sons of disobedience. Therefore do not be partakers with them.

For you were once darkness, but now you are light in the Lord. Walk as children of light (for the fruit of the Spirit is in all goodness, righteousness, and truth), finding out what is acceptable to the Lord. (Eph. 5:1–10)

The apostle declares that as holy ones of God, saints of the Lord, we are no longer darkness. We are now light in the Lord. That new identity works itself out in a changed life of holiness. Our point of reference is God and what pleases Him (see Paul's prayer toward this end in Col. 1:9–15).

The church is holy in this sense as it reflects a new orientation, a new morality, an oasis of grace in the midst of a world in rebellion against God. The ethos of the church is countercultural to that of the world. We want to remember that the church is not a building; it is a people. So when we say that we believe in a holy church, we are acknowledging a people holy to the Lord.

This brings us to an even more basic understanding of holiness. It does have to do with morals and behavior, but these flow out of a new status. The passages above reflect a before and an after. The Holy Spirit has delivered us from darkness and brought us into the light as the people of God. Peter addresses this corporate dimension of being separated out to God: "But you are a chosen generation, a royal priesthood, a holy nation, His own special people, that you may proclaim the praises of Him who called you out of darkness into His marvelous light; who once were not a people but are now the people of God, who had not obtained mercy but now have obtained mercy" (1 Peter 2:9–10). In the most basic sense, the church is holy because it is a people purchased for God by the blood of Christ and inhabited by God through the presence of the Holy Spirit. From the holiness of being separated to belong to God flows the holiness of purity and differentness from the world. We can see both aspects of being holy and the call to holiness in Paul's greeting to the church at Corinth: "To the church of God which is at Corinth, to those who are sanctified in Christ Jesus, called to be saints, with all who in every place call on the name of Jesus Christ our Lord, both theirs and ours" (1 Cor. 1:2). The root of the words "sanctified" and "saints" is the word *holy*. The church is holy by the action of God, to be holy by the call of God, and is ultimately holy because the holy God dwells in its midst.

The word for *church* in the New Testament is *ecclesia*. Technically, the word means "called out." The people of God are called-out ones. But if we were to form our understanding of the church on the basis of this one word, our understanding would be incomplete. *Ecclesia* translates a word from the Old Testament that means "gathered" or "assembled." While Christians are called out of the world, they are gathered together as the people of God.

When we confess in the Creed that we believe in a church that is holy, we testify to the work of God to form a people whose charter is Christ and whose character reflects that reality.

Catholic

I attended a church recently that included congregational recitation of the Apostles' Creed in its order of service, but I noticed they had changed one word. In the text printed in the bulletin the word *catholic* had been replaced with the word *universal*. Sometimes churches will include *universal* in parentheses or as a footnote to the word choice of the Creed. Over the years, I have had members of my congregation express confusion, thinking we as Protestants were aligning ourselves with the Roman Catholic Church.

The Creed is not taking a denominational stand by using the word *catholic*. Notice, in the first place, that the word does not begin with a capital letter but with a lowercase one: "the holy, catholic church." The word *catholic* simply means worldwide or global, not only in geography but across generations. Believing in a catholic church says we believe that the church is bigger than just the local church. Many of the letters of the New Testament are addressed to specific churches, such as the church in Corinth or the church in Philippi. They did not have buildings like we tend to think of today. Often churches met in homes. For example, in his letter to the church at Rome, Paul spoke of the church that met in the home of two of his coworkers, Priscilla and Aquila. Those local churches would have a visible form, with elders and activities and practices. They are the church, and the letters written to them are also written to us as the church.

The *catholic* church, however, speaks to the bigger church. God's people are spread throughout the world and throughout the ages. One beautiful picture of the makeup of this universal church can be found in the book of Revelation. The apostle John begins with a focus on Jesus Christ in His saving work to form a people belonging to God, a worshiping people. Writing to seven local churches in Asia Minor, he says: "To Him who loved us and washed us from our sins in His own blood, and has made us kings and priests to His God and Father, to Him be glory and dominion forever and ever. Amen" (Rev. 1:5–6). A bit later in the letter John gives us an idea of the diversity and breadth of this people:

> And they sang a new song, saying:
>
>> "You are worthy to take the scroll,
>> And to open its seals;
>> For You were slain,
>> And have redeemed us to God by Your blood
>> Out of every tribe and tongue and people and
>>   nation,
>> And have made us kings and priests to our God."
>>   (Rev. 5:9–10)

We see a beautiful picture of a diverse people bound together by the love of God and the blood of Christ, through the Holy Spirit.

God's plan from the start was to form a people for His own possession. Way back in Genesis God told Abraham that he would be a blessing to all the nations. In fact, Peter's descriptions of the church that we saw earlier (see 1 Peter 2:1–12) were first applied to God's people Israel in the Old

Testament. God's plan from the beginning, though, was for the nations, *both* Jews and Gentiles. God makes a remarkable statement through the Old Testament prophet Isaiah. To appreciate this statement it is helpful to know that Israel was comprised of Jews, and Egypt and Assyria were comprised of Gentiles. More than that, Egypt and Assyria were enemies of Israel, both serving as captors and oppressors to the Jews. The Jews came out of captivity in Egypt at their formation as a nation and were taken into captivity as a nation by the Assyrians. But here is what God says of the makeup of His people and His plan:

> In that day there will be a highway from Egypt to Assyria, and the Assyrian will come into Egypt and the Egyptian into Assyria, and the Egyptians will serve with the Assyrians.
>
> In that day Israel will be one of three with Egypt and Assyria—a blessing in the midst of the land, whom the LORD of hosts shall bless, saying, "Blessed is Egypt My people, and Assyria the work of My hands, and Israel My inheritance." (Isa. 19:23–25)

God's church is comprised of people across lands, across the ages, all undeserving but all blessed by God in Christ.

The church, whether in its local expression or its widespread extension, is a worshiping community in relationship with the living God. Though there are different ways of going about it, churches all around the world will reflect the distinctive of being holy to God and being charged with carrying out His mission for them. The Bible will be taught. People will be active in prayer. Songs of praise will echo from Christians gathered together for worship. The Creed gives us a sense of being part of something bigger than ourselves, bigger than our local body of believers. That sense protects us from pride we might derive from the size of our own congregation or discouragement because we feel isolated or alone or inadequate. The church is Christ's church, in which He lives by His Spirit. Jesus is building His church, and the gates of hell cannot stand against His work. That church becomes visible when unbelievers take refuge in Jesus's saving work and bow the knee before Him as Lord of their lives. They are pronounced by their profession, included in reciting the Apostles' Creed. The catholicity of the church in its unity and diversity is reflected by the hymn writer:

> Elect from every nation,
> Yet one o'er all the earth,
> Her charter of salvation,
> One Lord, one faith, one birth;
> One holy name she blesses,
> Partakes one holy food,
> And to one hope she presses,
> With ev'ry grace endued.[1]

Communion of Saints

Saints is another way of saying Christians. Many of the New Testament letters are addressed to the saints. For example, Paul salutes the Colossians in this way: "To the saints and faithful brethren in Christ who are in Colosse: Grace to you and peace from God our Father and the Lord Jesus Christ" (Col. 1:2). A saint does not refer to a special class of Christian. Rather, a saint is a believer. In the case of letters to churches, Paul is writing to groups of believers that comprise

---

1. Samuel J. Stone, "The Church's One Foundation," in the public domain.

local churches. This is in evidence in his second letter to the church at Corinth: "Paul, an apostle of Jesus Christ by the will of God, and Timothy our brother, to the church of God which is at Corinth, with all the saints who are in all Achaia" (1:1). Achaia was the southern region of Greece while Corinth was the capital and where the congregation of believers was located.

Here are three scenarios that help us to understand the communion of saints. The first is an inheritance. My wife, Linda, is one of six children. When her widowed mom died, the estate was divided among her and her siblings, each receiving an equal share. She, her four brothers, and her sister shared in the common inheritance.

The second scenario involves a performance. I attended a talent show during a family week at Harvey Cedars Bible Conference in New Jersey. There were two groups: those in the audience and those who were part of the show, those who participated and those who did not. I was in the former group. I would have participated, but I'm not sure puns can be classified as a talent. My group watched and enjoyed the various performers who sang or played an instrument or juggled or told stories.

The third scenario is of a business. Two men decided to start an office products business, not a storefront but one that sold and delivered to organizations. They became partners. The bulk of their interaction revolved around their venture together, with the goal of making their business succeed. Their bond was the business they shared. They shared responsibilities related to the running of the business and they shared in the profits together.

These three scenarios provide us with different perspectives on the *communion* of saints. The inheritance spoke of the benefits the heirs *shared* in together. The talent show spoke to the community and activity the performers *participated* in together. The business venture spoke to the *partnership* that bound the men together and directed their activity. All these words—*share, participate, partner*—are found in the Bible and translate the same word, *koinonia. Koinonia* is also translated "fellowship" or "communion." It refers to a common bond and a common expression of that bond. It speaks to a community dynamic, rooted in participation with Christ in the Spirit from which flows the fruit of new life. To believe in the communion of saints is to believe in this bond among Christians.

We can see this communion expressed in a variety of ways. In the Creed, belief in the communion of saints falls under the heading of belief in the Holy Spirit. Earlier we were reminded that the Spirit works in conjunction with Christ, uniting us to Jesus to partake of all His benefits. This position of participation in Christ is foundational to living out productive lives in Christ. Notice the unity of communion and its outworking in Paul's letter to the saints at Ephesus:

> I, therefore, the prisoner of the Lord, beseech you to walk worthy of the calling with which you were called, with all lowliness and gentleness, with longsuffering, bearing with one another in love, endeavoring to keep the unity of the Spirit in the bond of peace. There is one body and one Spirit, just as you were called in one hope of your calling; one Lord, one faith, one baptism; one God and Father of all, who is above all, and through all, and in you all. (4:1–6)

Although the word *koinonia* is not explicitly used here, we see its expression in the objective bond of the Spirit, the mandate to live out that bond, and what that bond looks like in life together.

Our communion is with Christ and with one another. Sometimes the Lord's Supper is called Communion. Celebration of the sacrament looks to our participation in the saving work of Jesus, and not just individually but in communion with one another who share a kindred faith. Prior to writing about the institution of the Lord's Supper in 1 Corinthians 11, Paul attests to the objective bond in 1 Corinthians 10:16–17: "The cup of blessing which we bless, is it not the communion of the blood of Christ? The bread which we break, is it not the communion of the body of Christ? For we, though many, are one bread and one body; for we all partake of that one bread." The communion of saints is first and foremost a communion with Christ in His saving work (see 1 Cor. 1:9; 1 John 1:3), a communion we share with others.

That objective participation with Christ makes demands on us that we live it out in our personal walk and relationships. In the Ephesians passage above we are called to live in keeping with our calling and in concert with fellow believers. Like insulin to a properly functioning body, humility is the grace that keeps us in proper position while love serves as the adrenaline. Since we are united to Christ and united in Christ, we are to be governed by the mind of Christ:

> Therefore if there is any consolation in Christ, if any comfort of love, if any fellowship of the Spirit, if any affection and mercy, fulfill my joy by being like-minded, having the same love, being of one accord, of one mind. Let nothing be done through selfish ambition or

conceit, but in lowliness of mind let each esteem others better than himself. Let each of you look out not only for his own interests, but also for the interests of others.

Let this mind be in you which was also in Christ Jesus. (Phil. 2:1–5)

This Philippians passage goes on to speak of the suffering of Christ, even to death on a cross. Suffering is another area that flows out of communion with Christ. Paul speaks of *koinonia* in Christ's sufferings. By bearing the name of Jesus, we don't suffer as Jesus did in His innocence under Pontius Pilate, but we do endure opposition from sinful men and undergo the miseries of a world antagonistic to the light. And we endure together. The whole tone of Peter's first letter has to do with suffering for the sake of Christ. Here is the Spirit's counsel to us who share in Christ's sufferings:

> Beloved, do not think it strange concerning the fiery trial which is to try you, as though some strange thing happened to you; but rejoice to the extent that you partake of Christ's sufferings, that when His glory is revealed, you may also be glad with exceeding joy. If you are reproached for the name of Christ, blessed are you, for the Spirit of glory and of God rests upon you. On their part He is blasphemed, but on your part He is glorified. But let none of you suffer as a murderer, a thief, an evildoer, or as a busybody in other people's matters. Yet if anyone suffers as a Christian, let him not be ashamed, but let him glorify God in this matter....
>
> Therefore let those who suffer according to the will of God commit their souls to Him in doing good, as to a faithful Creator. (1 Peter 4:12–16, 19)

For centuries, Christians have suffered for the gospel, even to the point of death.

The communion of saints has to do with our objective bond in Christ by His Spirit and the subjective expression of that bond individually and in community. One other aspect has to do with being part of a bigger context into which God has placed us by His Spirit. Fellowship in the Spirit leads to partnership in the gospel. Sometimes when we hear the word *fellowship*, our minds can go to social activity with other Christians, likely involving food. But fellowship is a far richer concept. The activity of fellowship is not just social but spiritual, not just eating but edifying and encouraging. When we get together with other believers, we want to put into practice all those "one another" passages we find in the Bible where we serve, love, exhort, admonish, rebuke, encourage, bear burdens, and build up one another in the Lord.

Another facet of our communion in Christ by which we bless and serve one another is depicted by a body. A body has arms, legs, feet, eyes, and the like. The apostle Paul writes this to the fractured church at Corinth: "There are diversities of gifts, but the same Spirit. There are differences of ministries, but the same Lord. And there are diversities of activities, but it is the same God who works all in all. But the manifestation of the Spirit is given to each one for the profit of all" (1 Cor. 12:4–7). Gifts, talents, and abilities are not for self-promotion but to promote the health, wholeness, and operation of the body. When Paul spoke of one Lord and one Spirit to the church at Ephesus, he went on to speak of different gifts believers bring to the table for the good of the whole (Eph. 4:11–16). He does the same to the church at Corinth, as we see further on in chapter 12:

> For as the body is one and has many members, but all the members of that one body, being many, are

one body, so also is Christ. For by one Spirit we were all baptized into one body—whether Jews or Greeks, whether slaves or free—and have all been made to drink into one Spirit. For in fact the body is not one member but many.

If the foot should say, "Because I am not a hand, I am not of the body," is it therefore not of the body? And if the ear should say, "Because I am not an eye, I am not of the body," is it therefore not of the body? If the whole body were an eye, where would be the hearing? If the whole were hearing, where would be the smelling? But now God has set the members, each one of them, in the body just as He pleased. And if they were all one member, where would the body be?

But now indeed there are many members, yet one body. (1 Cor. 12:12–20)

Gifts, talents, and abilities are governed by *koinonia*, by the communion of saints indwelt by the Spirit and endowed by the Spirit for the sake of Christ. My five-year-old grandson Asher is a sliver of a boy, slight and wiry. He loves to do jigsaw puzzles. Unlike his older siblings, he will devote the time and concentration necessary to put together some pretty involved puzzles. A jigsaw puzzle is made up of many irregular and unique pieces that fit together to form a single picture. Asher will take a piece in hand and find its spot.

That is God's design for us in the communion of saints. Each of us is distinct and part of the whole for the functioning of the body. No one piece is more important than another. Those pieces that are involved in public speaking do not have a greater honor than those involved in behind-the-scenes chores driven by a servant's heart. How do we find our niche? We involve ourselves. We see where God satisfies us.

We look and listen to find where God is particularly blessing our efforts. Often, it is through the feedback of others we discover that blessing. Not that we need to serve only where we perceive ourselves to have a spiritual talent. Often, we serve simply where needed, for the common good.

The communion of saints is formed and fueled by the Holy Spirit. Peter presents us with grand masterpieces of grace in the outworking of this *koinonia* (e.g., 1 Peter 3:8–12), but we close this section with a picture that depicts what gospel life is all about in Christ's church:

> And above all things have fervent love for one another, for "love will cover a multitude of sins." Be hospitable to one another without grumbling. As each one has received a gift, minister it to one another, as good stewards of the manifold grace of God. If anyone speaks, let him speak as the oracles of God. If anyone ministers, let him do it as with the ability which God supplies, that in all things God may be glorified through Jesus Christ, to whom belong the glory and the dominion forever and ever. Amen. (1 Peter 4:8–11)

To believe in the holy, catholic church, the communion of saints, is to belong to Christ and one another and to long for His glory together.

9

THE FORGIVENESS OF SINS

I believe in…the forgiveness of sins.

The Apostles' Creed now turns to the blessings of salvation in Christ, summed up in the forgiveness of sins and eternal life, blessings shared by the communion of saints. The church is the redeemed of the Lord, ransomed by the blood of Christ, reserved for eternal communion with Him. The prophet Isaiah whets our appetite with these words of promise and grace:

> And the ransomed of the LORD shall return,
> And come to Zion with singing,
> With everlasting joy on their heads.
> They shall obtain joy and gladness,
> And sorrow and sighing shall flee away. (Isa. 35:10)

Everlasting joy belongs to the redeemed of the Lord.

To *redeem* means to "buy back." A pastor went to downtown Philadelphia to visit an ailing friend. Parking is a nightmare in Philly, but he finally found a spot. He parked his car and walked the block to his friend's home. Less than an hour later he was back at his car—or where his car should have been. His first thought was that it had been stolen, but then he noticed the sign: "No parking after 5 p.m." The sign conveniently gave the phone number of the towing service. He pulled out his cell phone and called the number, and sure enough, they had his car. He was told the tow truck was just bringing it in. He paid for a taxi to make the trek across town. He approached the employee seated behind an inch-thick Plexiglas window and asked for his car. He was told that would be 230 dollars. Realizing that pleading, reasoning, and threatening weren't getting him anywhere, he paid the extortion and left with his car. He redeemed his car. He paid the ransom, buying it back at no small cost.[1]

Earlier we saw in the magisterial sentence of Ephesians 1 that God has blessed us with every spiritual blessing in Christ. At the heart of that sentence we read, "In Him we have redemption through His blood, the forgiveness of sins, according to the riches of His grace" (Eph. 1:7). Redemption relates to the forgiveness of sins. The cost to redeem that pastor's car was exorbitant. The cost to pay the debt of our sin was incalculable.

Forgiveness of sins brings us to the crux of the gospel and the beating heart of the church as the redeemed of the Lord. The church is a community of those forgiven, of those who practice forgiveness, and of those who proclaim forgiveness. We now turn to each of these aspects to gain an understanding of the glory of the grace of forgiveness highlighted by the Apostles' Creed.

---

1. This illustration is adapted from an August 2017 talk by Dr. Charles Zimmerman.

Forgiveness

Forgiveness implies a wrong. The Bible expresses it in terms of debt. How do we know our wrong and calculate our debt? By the law of God, the Ten Commandments. If we hold our lives up to the mirror of God's law, we see ourselves covered with the grime of sin's guilt. We violate God's law in thought, word, and deed, doing what it forbids and not doing what it bids. The religious leaders of Jesus's day believed themselves to be law keepers, meticulously trying to obey God's commands. Jesus, however, held up the mirror of the law to them and turned on the bright lights of illumination so they could see themselves more plainly. They thought they had kept the commandment not to murder because they had never killed anyone. But Jesus said that if they had held anger in their heart they had broken that commandment, stood guilty for it, and were condemned because of it. All of us see that same reflection.

Paul makes Jesus's point by indicting all humanity in declaring, "All have sinned and fall short of the glory of God" (Rom. 3:23). It's not just those pompous, presumptuous religious leaders that Jesus was indicting. All of us have broken God's law, stand guilty for it, and are condemned because of it. We cannot measure up to God's demands for perfect obedience, nor can we make up for the wrongs we have done. The condemnation of the law breaker rests on our heads. As Paul puts it in his letter to the Galatians: "For as many as are of the works of the law are under the curse; for it is written, 'Cursed is everyone who does not continue in all things which are written in the book of the law, to do them'" (3:10).

It is against this backdrop of standing before the judgment seat of God—guilty, vile, and helpless—that the good news of the gospel of Jesus Christ resounds with such glory and delight. But being acquitted by God is one thing; being acceptable to Him is another.

Paul lays out the gospel most methodically in his letters to the Romans and Galatians. Yet in Romans the word *forgiveness* is mentioned only one time, and that in a quote from the Old Testament. In Galatians it is not mentioned at all. Forgiveness is God's answer to the debt of our sin, the outcome of our redemption, the centerpiece of the gospel of Jesus Christ, but it appears conspicuously absent in these letters that major on the gospel! How can that be?

Forgiveness is not absent in these letters; rather, it is packaged with something else necessary for us in respect to the law of God. That package is justification. Completing the thought of Romans 3:23–24 we find this: "For all have sinned and fall short of the glory of God, being justified freely by His grace through the redemption that is in Christ Jesus." We find the same thing in Galatians: "A man is not justified by the works of the law but by faith in Jesus Christ, even we have believed in Christ Jesus, that we might be justified by faith in Christ and not by the works of the law; for by the works of the law no flesh shall be justified" (2:16). The answer to sin is expressed in terms of justification.

The cost of forgiveness, the payment of sin's debt, is made by the sacrificial death of Jesus in the place of sinners, something we affirmed in the second section of the Apostles' Creed. At the cross, Christ paid the debt in full—not for His sins, for He had none, but for the sins of those He came to save. Paul grounds justification in the cross of Christ: "I do not set aside the grace of God; for if righteousness comes through the law, then Christ died in vain" (Gal. 2:21). In other words, if we could save ourselves by obedience to the law,

Christ's death was unnecessary. But no one can be forgiven by self-reformation or personal performance. As the apostle says, "No one is justified by the law in the sight of God" (Gal. 3:11). Christ took upon Himself the guilt of our sin and suffered the curse of the condemned in our place, the only hope of salvation for any sinner: "Christ has redeemed us from the curse of the law, having become a curse for us (for it is written, 'Cursed is everyone who hangs on a tree'), that the blessing of Abraham might come upon the Gentiles in Christ Jesus, that we might receive the promise of the Spirit through faith" (Gal. 3:13–14).

The redeeming work of Jesus purchased us for God by paying the ransom for our sin. The debt of our sin is neither ignored nor simply pardoned; it is paid in full. We receive that forgiveness by grace, through faith, enabled by the Holy Spirit, who unites us to Christ. The Spirit tunes our hearts to sing in humble astonishment:

> My sin—oh, the bliss of this glorious thought!—
> My sin, not in part, but the whole,
> Is nailed to the cross, and I bear it no more;
> Praise the Lord, praise the Lord, O my soul![2]

But there is more for us to be right with God, more good news of the gospel shared by the redeemed of the Lord. We mentioned that forgiveness of sins comes packaged in the blessing of justification. What else is in that package? Paul spells it out for us. After making it painfully clear that no one is righteous in the sight of God, he broadcasts this glorious news:

---

2. Horatio G. Spafford, "It Is Well with My Soul," in the public domain.

But now the righteousness of God apart from the law is revealed, being witnessed by the Law and the Prophets, even the righteousness of God, through faith in Jesus Christ, to all and on all who believe. For there is no difference; for all have sinned and fall short of the glory of God, being justified freely by His grace through the redemption that is in Christ Jesus, whom God set forth as a propitiation by His blood, through faith, to demonstrate His righteousness, because in His forbearance God had passed over the sins that were previously committed, to demonstrate at the present time His righteousness, that He might be just and the justifier of the one who has faith in Jesus. (Rom. 3:21–26)

The "now" of verse 21 is the now of fulfillment in the person and work of Jesus Christ. Through faith in Him we find what is necessary for sinners to be acquitted and acceptable to a holy God who will by no means leave the guilty unpunished. The package of justification contains forgiveness of sins and the garment of righteousness, both cleansing and clothing. Christ cleanses us from sin's stains and clothes us with His spotless righteousness—the great exchange of grace. Sinners find acceptance before a holy God through Jesus, who gave His life on the cross to atone for their sin and who gives His life of sinless obedience to their credit.

Practicing Forgiveness

By grace alone, through faith alone, in Christ alone Christians stand forgiven. By Christ's work on our behalf, we are declared not guilty and pronounced spotlessly righteous because of Jesus's record of perfect obedience credited to us. Justification involves a one-time pronouncement by God.

That's why the apostle Paul can say, "There is therefore now no condemnation to those who are in Christ Jesus" (Rom. 8:1). Though God's forgiveness is comprehensive, dealing with all sins private and public; sins past, present, or future; sins intentional and unintentional, sin is not something behind us, not yet. We live in and live out that forgiveness on a daily basis, both in our personal walk with God and in our relationships within the household of faith. It is to each of these areas we turn in unpacking the forgiveness of sins we confess in the Creed.[3]

Living in the Grace of Forgiveness

John tells us in his first epistle that "if we confess our sins, [God] is faithful and just to forgive us our sins and to cleanse us from all unrighteousness" (1:9). That is wonderfully comforting to us. When we affirm with the Creed that we believe in the forgiveness of sins, this confidence in confession is part of that affirmation. But that raises a question: Why do we need to confess our sins if we are already forgiven? Didn't we just say that the totality of guilt of our sins was laid on Christ?

Perhaps John is writing to unbelievers, enticing them to Christ with the promise of forgiveness. But no, John is writing to Christians, those whose fellowship is with the Father and the Son, those he calls beloved children of God. In fact, the theme of the entire letter has to do with professing Christians knowing they are truly Christians. John lays out his purpose statement toward the close of his epistle: "These things

---

3. For more on this great transaction and for study of forgiveness and its practice, see Stanley D. Gale, *Finding Forgiveness: Discovering the Healing Power of the Gospel* (Grand Rapids: Reformation Heritage Books, 2016).

I have written to you who believe in the name of the Son of God, that you may know that you have eternal life, and that you may continue to believe in the name of the Son of God" (1 John 5:13). Clearly John is writing to believers to assure them of salvation and to shore up their faith in Christ.

Bracketing John's assurance in 1:9 that if we confess our sins we will find forgiveness is the equal assurance that we continue to sin. Before verse 9 we read, "If we say that we have no sin, we deceive ourselves, and the truth is not in us" (v. 8). John is even more emphatic following verse 9, where he says that if we do not admit we sin we call God a liar, and such denial is actually an indicator that we are not believers: "If we say that we have not sinned, we make Him a liar, and His word is not in us" (v. 10). Assurance of forgiveness through confession emerges from acknowledgment of continuing sin. So governed by the theme of the letter, awareness of continuing sin is one of the signs that we are truly believers.

Then why would one whose sin *is* forgiven need to confess in order *to be* forgiven? The answer has to do with communion with God. When we confess our sins, we do so not as guilty sinners to a righteous judge. We confess as adopted children to our heavenly Father. When I tell my children to do something and they disobey me, I don't stop being their father. But in their disobedience, they have rebelled against me. In like fashion, when we sin against God we turn our back on Him to follow after sin (John calls it idolatry in the last verse of his letter), and our communion with Him is hindered. Our relationship with God does not change. We remain His children, but our fellowship with Him is affected. When we acknowledge our sin, as straying children we turn to God to find not that He left us but we left Him, and we return to Him through confession that admits our wrong.

The assurance that John gives us for finding forgiveness when we confess our sin to God is that God is "faithful and just" to forgive us our sins. That should be a bit surprising to us. *Faithful* makes sense. God is true to His character and to His word. We can trust Him. But why *just*? We would expect John to say merciful rather than just, that God is faithful and merciful to forgive us our sins. When we are pulled over for speeding and found transgressing the law, we want mercy not justice, a warning not a ticket. Why is God *just* to forgive us? Our answer is found as John finishes the thought. "My little children, these things I write to you, so that you may not sin. And if anyone sins, we have an Advocate with the Father, Jesus Christ the righteous. And He Himself is the propitiation for our sins, and not for ours only but also for the whole world" (2:1–2). For the forgiveness of our sin, God points us to His justice, a justice that has been satisfied in Christ. What that means is that forgiveness of sins is not found in confession of sin but in confession of Christ. The forgiveness of sins in the third section of the Creed is founded on the work of Christ in the second section of the Creed. The fact that Christ is the means provided not only for us but for the whole world reminds us that there is only one way of salvation, one name given by God by which any can be saved.

John says something else intriguing related to forgiveness of sins. He says that when we confess our sin, God not only forgives that sin but "cleanses us from all unrighteousness." There are some who suggest that we need to keep short accounts with God by staying on top of confession of our sin. They go so far as to suggest that if we forget to confess a sin, it remains in our account and we are liable for it. That teaching is misguided at best, heretical at worst. It denies the gospel and the completed and comprehensive work of Jesus Christ on our behalf.

The image John uses of cleansing presents a wonderful picture. Sin is described in the Bible as something that soils us. Isaiah likened even our righteousness to filthy rags. There is a real sense that we need to repent not only of our sin but also of our righteousness, if we think that righteousness commends us in any way to God and that we need Christ less than someone else. Even our best of intentions are tainted by sin. Only Christ was pure.

The concept of cleansing appeals to us when we wander from God to wallow in the mud of some sin. Like a nice shower washes away the dirt and grime after a ten-mile forest hike, so we relate to confession cleansing us from the grit and mire of sin. But we would be better served to understand the impact of Christ's work by thinking in terms of the debt our sin creates. Instead of confession involving a wash basin, we might consider an accounting ledger. When we confess a sin, it is as though we open a record of our sin. We turn to the page where the sin we are confessing is recorded and run our finger to the column beside it. There we find "paid in full." Our eyes scan the rest of the page, and beside each transgression are the words "paid in full." We flip back pages from dates prior and see the same notation beside every debt of sin. We flip ahead to every sin of the entirety of our lives and find the same notification. Every sin is accounted for and all the debt satisfied through the payment of the cross. When we confess our sin, we confess not to gain forgiveness but to find forgiveness already procured through Christ and Him crucified. In Him we are cleansed from *all* unrighteousness.

Confession of sin should be part of our daily practice, a feature of our life of prayer in communion with our God. Psalms 32 and 51 and others serve as examples of confession upon awareness of sin. But the particular joy of confession comes in rekindling awareness of the love of God in the gospel of His Son. The Holy Spirit ministers grace to our sin-weary souls and renews us in the righteousness, joy, and peace that are ours through Jesus Christ.

Living Out the Grace of Forgiveness

"Behold, how good and how pleasant it is for brethren to dwell together in unity!" (Ps. 133:1). How sweet it is not only to be at peace with God but also with others! Our Lord puts a premium on such peace. In His High Priestly Prayer of John 17, He prays for peace, both for the sake of the glory of God and for testimony to the world:

> I do not pray for these alone, but also for those who will believe in Me through their word; that they all may be one, as You, Father, are in Me, and I in You; that they also may be one in Us, that the world may believe that You sent Me. And the glory which You gave Me I have given them, that they may be one just as We are one: I in them, and You in Me; that they may be made perfect in one, and that the world may know that You have sent Me, and have loved them as You have loved Me. (vv. 17:20–23)

The unity Jesus prayed for is never at the expense of truth, but in the cause of truth. Paul describes how truth and love function toward unity: "But, speaking the truth in love,

[we] may grow up in all things into Him who is the head—Christ—from whom the whole body, joined and knit together by what every joint supplies, according to the effective working by which every part does its share, causes growth of the body for the edifying of itself in love" (Eph. 4:15–16). Love exerts the gravitational pull of truth toward unity.

Forgiveness is one of the means God gives us for achieving and maintaining peace in relationships. Paul sets the tone for life in Christ's church:

> Therefore, as the elect of God, holy and beloved, put on tender mercies, kindness, humility, meekness, long-suffering; bearing with one another, and forgiving one another, if anyone has a complaint against another; even as Christ forgave you, so you also must do. But above all these things put on love, which is the bond of perfection. And let the peace of God rule in your hearts, to which also you were called in one body; and be thankful. Let the word of Christ dwell in you richly in all wisdom, teaching and admonishing one another in psalms and hymns and spiritual songs, singing with grace in your hearts to the Lord. And whatever you do in word or deed, do all in the name of the Lord Jesus, giving thanks to God the Father through Him. (Col. 3:12–17)

Forgiving one another is God's way of preserving unity and promoting truth. Offenses, grievances, and complaints all have the potential to divide and destroy. Forgiveness does not allow those things a foothold. The "root of bitterness" that can spring up (Heb. 12:15) not only threatens us in our inner being but acts to defile *many* and so promote disunity. In the model prayer He gave His disciples, Jesus taught the central place of forgiveness in the lives of those who have been forgiven. We are to forgive those in our debt as we have been forgiven. Our forgiveness in Christ sets the tone for our dealing with others in our debt of wrong.

How do we live out such forgiveness? How do we become peacemakers who seek to preserve the communion of the saints in relationship with one another? It all starts with appreciating God's forgiveness of us and applying that toward others. Our Lord Jesus gives that point of reference in a parable:

> Therefore the kingdom of heaven is like a certain king who wanted to settle accounts with his servants. And when he had begun to settle accounts, one was brought to him who owed him ten thousand talents. But as he was not able to pay, his master commanded that he be sold, with his wife and children and all that he had, and that payment be made. The servant therefore fell down before him, saying, "Master, have patience with me, and I will pay you all." Then the master of that servant was moved with compassion, released him, and forgave him the debt.
>
> But that servant went out and found one of his fellow servants who owed him a hundred denarii; and he laid hands on him and took him by the throat, saying, "Pay me what you owe!" So his fellow servant fell down at his feet and begged him, saying, "Have patience with me, and I will pay you all." And he would not, but went and threw him into prison till he should pay the debt. So when his fellow servants saw what had been done, they were very grieved, and came and told their master all that had been done. Then his master, after he had called him, said to him, "You wicked servant! I forgave you all that debt because you begged me. Should you not also have had compassion on your fellow servant,

just as I had pity on you?" And his master was angry, and delivered him to the torturers until he should pay all that was due to him.

So My heavenly Father also will do to you if each of you, from his heart, does not forgive his brother his trespasses. (Matt. 18:23–35)

The story is shocking in a number of ways. No doubt that was Jesus's intention in order to make sure we don't miss the point. The very idea of a servant being able to amass such a mind-boggling debt to the king is outlandish. But that's where Jesus starts us, the point of reference He gives us. A denarius was a day's wage. The second servant owed one hundred denarii, about three months' wages. The first servant owed ten thousand talents. Based on a denarius a day, that would equal about 160,000 years' wages. To think that the first servant refused to forgive a relative pittance in light of the forgiveness of his insurmountable debt was shocking. We would get upset if we gave one of our children one thousand pennies and that child refused to give one to a friend.

This parable primes us for forgiving as we have been forgiven. God released us from our ocean of debt against Him and so we should readily release others from their puddle of debt against us. Jesus presents a double conclusion, one to the parable and one to the overall teaching. His first is in verse 33 in the king's statement to his servant: "Should you not also have had compassion on your fellow servant, just as I had pity on you?" In verse 34, after discovering the servant's double standard and refusal to forgive, we are told that "his master was angry, and delivered him to the torturers until he should pay all that was due to him." The second conclusion comes in verse 35 and seems to give us cause for alarm.

Then Jesus says, "So My heavenly Father also will do to you if each of you, from his heart, does not forgive his brother his trespasses."

Is Jesus saying that God's forgiveness can be rescinded, that the debt of our sin could be restored if we don't forgive others? For that matter, God demands forgiveness *from the heart*. What if my heart is not in it—or in it enough? We want to note that this parable is not intended to present a complete picture of the gospel. There is no mediator between the king and the one who owes him the massive debt, no one to pay the debt on his behalf. Jesus is making the simple point in verse 33 that we are to forgive as we have been forgiven.

The point of the parable concerns the boundaries of forgiveness. Jesus addresses those boundaries in answer to Peter's question that prompted the parable:

> Then Peter came to Him and said, "Lord, how often shall my brother sin against me, and I forgive him? Up to seven times?"
>
> Jesus said to him, "I do not say to you, up to seven times, but up to seventy times seven." (Matt. 18:21–22)

The parable explains why Jesus told Peter he was to forgive seventy times seven. Peter thought he was being magnanimous in forgiving seven times, but Jesus gives Peter a whole new way of accounting. He describes an unreasonable grace that God has lavished upon us, grace without boundaries, grace that superabounds. In our dealings with others who have sinned against us, the image is of the floodwaters of God's grace to us overflowing their banks in our forgiveness to others.

When Jesus spoke of the unforgiving servant being handed over to torturers for repayment of debt and said,

"So My heavenly Father also will do to you if each of you, from his heart, does not forgive his brother his trespasses" in verse 35, He was not saying that our debt of forgiven sin could be reinstated by God so that we face condemnation. Rather, He was awakening us to dread of unforgiven sin. So Jesus compels us to forgive by reminding us of God's grace to us in His forgiveness of a debt we could not pay and by reminding us of the horror of being held prisoner to sin's debt. When we say in the Apostles' Creed that we believe in the forgiveness of sins, we affirm the gospel of Jesus Christ, and we commit ourselves to forgive as we have been forgiven.

Proclaiming Forgiveness

Believing in forgiveness of sins also touches on the mission of the holy, catholic church in carrying out the work of Christ to build His church. The church is not a static institution. It is a dynamic enterprise alive and striving through the power of the Holy Spirit for the sake of Christ's kingdom. Before His ascension Jesus told His followers, "But you shall receive power when the Holy Spirit has come upon you; and you shall be witnesses to Me in Jerusalem, and in all Judea and Samaria, and to the end of the earth" (Acts 1:8). That witness is to Jesus as the Christ and the forgiveness of sins gained by faith in Him.

After His resurrection but before His ascension, Jesus met with two of His disciples on the road to Emmaus. He explained that He is the fulfillment of the whole of the Old Testament (see also John 5:36–40). He then went on to describe the mission and the message:

Then He said to them, "These are the words which I spoke to you while I was still with you, that all things must be fulfilled which were written in the Law of Moses and the Prophets and the Psalms concerning Me." And He opened their understanding, that they might comprehend the Scriptures.

Then He said to them, "Thus it is written, and thus it was necessary for the Christ to suffer and to rise from the dead the third day, and that repentance and remission of sins should be preached in His name to all nations, beginning at Jerusalem." (Luke 24:44–47)

The news to be heralded among the nations was the forgiveness of sins. Like broadcasting that a cancer has been cured, the remedy to a far more insidious and widespread affliction was to be proclaimed. Forgiveness of sins had not been discovered but accomplished through Him who bore sin's scourge and broke its bonds.

With the promise fulfilled and the Spirit given, the book of Acts records the church embarking on its gospel mission, beginning at Jerusalem: "Then Peter said to them, 'Repent, and let every one of you be baptized in the name of Jesus Christ for the remission of sins; and you shall receive the gift of the Holy Spirit. For the promise is to you and to your children, and to all who are afar off, as many as the Lord our God will call'" (Acts 2:38–39). This message of forgiveness of sins and deliverance from death winds its way through the book:

Him God has exalted to His right hand to be Prince and Savior, to give repentance to Israel and forgiveness of sins. And we are His witnesses to these things, and so also is the Holy Spirit whom God has given to those who obey Him. (5:31–32)

> To Him all the prophets witness that, through His name, whoever believes in Him will receive remission of sins. (10:43)

> Therefore let it be known to you, brethren, that through this Man is preached to you the forgiveness of sins; and by Him everyone who believes is justified from all things from which you could not be justified by the law of Moses. (13:38–39)

> To open [the Gentiles'] eyes, in order to turn them from darkness to light, and from the power of Satan to God, that they may receive forgiveness of sins and an inheritance among those who are sanctified by faith in Me. (26:18)

Not only is the message of forgiveness of sins to be proclaimed to the nations but it is to be perpetuated in the church. The gospel is to be preached for the evangelization of the unbeliever but also for the edification of the believer. We tend to forget, to think ourselves less needy of Christ, more deserving than others—to think that we contribute somehow to our salvation, that a few threads of our own are sewn among those of Christ in our garment of righteousness. But our salvation from sin's curse is all of Christ, only of Christ.

To counteract our forgetfulness, our Lord gives us a sacrament that is to be observed regularly. As we break the bread and drink from the cup, our eyes are lifted to Christ, remembering His death until He comes again:

> And as they were eating, Jesus took bread, blessed and broke it, and gave it to the disciples and said, "Take, eat; this is My body."
> Then He took the cup, and gave thanks, and gave it to them, saying, "Drink from it, all of you. For this is

My blood of the new covenant, which is shed for many for the remission [forgiveness] of sins." (Matt. 26:26–28)

This sacrament, however, will not be celebrated forever. The Lord's Supper is to be observed until Christ returns. It is to this future glory that the Creed now leads us.

10

RESURRECTION TO LIFE EVERLASTING

I believe in...the resurrection of the body,
and the life everlasting.

I am a tennis player and a Roger Federer fan. More often than not, I am unable to watch his matches. So I record them. Whether I actually watch the recording depends on one thing—if he wins. I'm not one of those who doesn't want to spoil things by avoiding news of the outcome. I don't want to watch to see if he wins. I want to watch him win. That's why when he loses games or seems to be struggling, I don't need to be worried because I know he wins the match.

That outlook is carried into the final two declarations of the Apostles' Creed. Both the resurrection of the body and the life everlasting are done deals, certainties for those who can say with genuine faith, "I believe." Christ has won, and those who rest in Him are more than conquerors. The book of Revelation gives us great encouragement for the battles now because it assures us that the war has been waged and won by Him who sits on the throne. Paul strikes this note in his letter to the Romans:

The Spirit Himself bears witness with our spirit that we are children of God, and if children, then heirs—heirs of God and joint heirs with Christ, if indeed we suffer with Him, that we may also be glorified together.

For I consider that the sufferings of this present time are not worthy to be compared with the glory which shall be revealed in us. (8:16–18)

The Creed ends on a high note for those whose hope is the Lord. In this chapter we climb the lofty mountain of God's grace to stand at the vista of eternity and behold what God has in store for those who love Him.

Resurrection of the Body

I've often wondered if Jesus did Lazarus a disservice by raising him from the dead (John 11). Certainly Lazarus *was* raised from the dead and emerged from the tomb to meet his Savior, who had called him by name. No doubt Lazarus's sisters, Mary and Martha, were thrilled to be reunited with their brother. But the reason I wonder is based on Paul's statement to the Philippians: "For to me, to live is Christ, and to die is gain. But if I live on in the flesh, this will mean fruit from my labor; yet what I shall choose I cannot tell. For I am hard-pressed between the two, having a desire to depart and be with Christ, which is far better" (1:21–23). Did Jesus deprive Lazarus of the better thing? I suppose, just as with Paul, God still had plans for Lazarus as His servant.

The Bible teaches that Christians who die go immediately to be with their Lord, who died for them and lives for them. But God has more in store. He has bigger plans for Lazarus, and He does for us as well. Lazarus's body would one day die again. In fact, the religious leaders looked for ways to make that happen sooner rather than later (John 12:10). But Lazarus and all whose hope is Christ can look forward to receiving resurrection bodies that are not subject to sickness, pain, or death. Paul whets our appetites: "For our citizenship is in heaven, from which we also eagerly wait for the Savior, the Lord Jesus Christ, who will transform our lowly body that it may be conformed to His glorious body, according to the working by which He is able even to subdue all things to Himself" (Phil. 3:20–21).

When the Apostles' Creed speaks of the resurrection of the body, it looks to this transformation. The most detailed account of the resurrection body itself is given by Paul to the church at Corinth. It is a lengthy passage, but it reads like an action adventure. And it is biographical, showing us a chapter of our lives we have yet to experience but which is already written for us by the hand of our God:

> But someone will say, "How are the dead raised up? And with what body do they come?" Foolish one, what you sow is not made alive unless it dies. And what you sow, you do not sow that body that shall be, but mere grain— perhaps wheat or some other grain. But God gives it a body as He pleases, and to each seed its own body.
>
> All flesh is not the same flesh, but there is one kind of flesh of men, another flesh of animals, another of fish, and another of birds.
>
> There are also celestial bodies and terrestrial bodies; but the glory of the celestial is one, and the glory of the terrestrial is another. There is one glory of the sun, another glory of the moon, and another glory of the stars; for one star differs from another star in glory.
>
> So also is the resurrection of the dead. The body is sown in corruption, it is raised in incorruption.

It is sown in dishonor, it is raised in glory. It is sown in weakness, it is raised in power. It is sown a natural body, it is raised a spiritual body. There is a natural body, and there is a spiritual body. And so it is written, "The first man Adam became a living being." The last Adam became a life-giving spirit.

However, the spiritual is not first, but the natural, and afterward the spiritual. The first man was of the earth, made of dust; the second Man is the Lord from heaven. As was the man of dust, so also are those who are made of dust; and as is the heavenly Man, so also are those who are heavenly. And as we have borne the image of the man of dust, we shall also bear the image of the heavenly Man.

Now this I say, brethren, that flesh and blood cannot inherit the kingdom of God; nor does corruption inherit incorruption. Behold, I tell you a mystery: We shall not all sleep, but we shall all be changed—in a moment, in the twinkling of an eye, at the last trumpet. For the trumpet will sound, and the dead will be raised incorruptible, and we shall be changed. For this corruptible must put on incorruption, and this mortal must put on immortality. So when this corruptible has put on incorruption, and this mortal has put on immortality, then shall be brought to pass the saying that is written: "Death is swallowed up in victory."

"O Death, where is your sting?

O Hades, where is your victory?"

The sting of death is sin, and the strength of sin is the law. But thanks be to God, who gives us the victory through our Lord Jesus Christ.

Therefore, my beloved brethren, be steadfast, immovable, always abounding in the work of the Lord,

knowing that your labor is not in vain in the Lord."
(1 Cor. 15:35–58)

This passage does not answer all our questions, such as
what age our bodies will be or what we will look like, but it
does answer the questions posed in verse 35 of how the dead
will be raised and what sort of body they will have. I have
read a number of arguments recently on the appropriate-
ness of cremation as opposed to bodily burial. It seems to me
Paul's instruction says that whether our bodies are ashes or
dust, they will be made new and indestructible.

We might note that when Paul describes the resurrection
body as spiritual and not flesh and blood (1 Cor. 15:44, 50),
he is not saying the resurrection body is immaterial, like a
ghost. He is saying that it is of the Holy Spirit. Again, we see
reference to the Holy Spirit and the blessings He brings us in
Christ. Here is how Paul expresses this reality of redemption
elsewhere:

> But you are not in the flesh but in the Spirit, if indeed
> the Spirit of God dwells in you. Now if anyone does not
> have the Spirit of Christ, he is not His. And if Christ is
> in you, the body is dead because of sin, but the Spirit is
> life because of righteousness. But if the Spirit of Him
> who raised Jesus from the dead dwells in you, He who
> raised Christ from the dead will also give life to your
> mortal bodies through His Spirit who dwells in you.
> (Rom. 8:9–11)

How exciting!

And what will our new body be like? The Bible gives us
an agricultural analogy. Farmers grow crops. When they go
to sell their crops, they don't pack up all the acres of produce.
They take a sample. That sample represents the entire crop

and shows its quality. Earlier in his defense of the resurrection of the body, Paul used that analogy: "But now Christ is risen from the dead, and has become the firstfruits of those who have fallen asleep" (1 Cor. 15:20). Jesus is the firstfruits in that more of the resurrection harvest is to come, and His resurrection body shows us what we can expect of our own.

A pastor friend of mine was an avid bicyclist. He would ride miles and miles at a time. One day he was out on the road when a car veered too close and nudged him into a ditch. He was never the same. He lost feeling and use of his whole body below the neck. He would be confined to a wheelchair the rest of his life. Thanks to innovative technology, he was able to do some things using his mouth and even tried to return to the pastorate. Also thankfully, his wife who had pledged her faithfulness in sickness and in health, till death they did part, stayed by his side. Most thankfully, my pastor friend can look forward to the unfettered freedom of an immortal and imperishable resurrection body when Jesus returns.

The resurrection of the body is a precious hope for Christians. It is also shared hope to be anticipated by all who are part of the communion of saints. In his second letter to the Corinthians, Paul lays out a poetic and encouraging expression of future hope in present reality. He describes our present bodies as "jars of clay," fragile and breakable:

> But we have this treasure in earthen vessels, that the excellence of the power may be of God and not of us. We are hard-pressed on every side, yet not crushed; we are perplexed, but not in despair; persecuted, but not forsaken; struck down, but not destroyed—always carrying about in the body the dying of the Lord Jesus,

that the life of Jesus also may be manifested in our
body. (4:7–10)

Those jars of clay will be replaced by bodies fit for eternity, as
Paul goes on to say: "He who raised up the Lord Jesus will also
raise us up with Jesus, and will present us with you" (4:14).
"Us" and "you"—if we are believers, *we* will together share in
Christ's glory, forever with our Lord.

Life Everlasting

The prospect of living forever can be an enticing one. The cos-
metic industry certainly tries its best to give an appearance of
youth. Modern medicine has helped to extend the average life
span. Yet with all that, people die. Their bodies wear out and
expire. As I have aged, I've noticed my strength and stam-
ina have waned. I know personally Paul's encouragement:
"Therefore we do not lose heart. Even though our outward
man is perishing, yet the inward man is being renewed day
by day. For our light affliction, which is but for a moment,
is working for us a far more exceeding and eternal weight
of glory, while we do not look at the things which are seen,
but at the things which are not seen. For the things which
are seen are temporary, but the things which are not seen
are eternal" (4:16–18). We live life now in the light of glory.
That glory anticipates a glorified body and a glorified existence. Momentary affliction, whether aches and pains or even
extreme suffering, will be swallowed up in eternity, where in
the fullness of the new creation there will be no more death,
disaster, or disease (Revelation 21). In the moment suffering may be intense and seem unending, but that will not be
the ultimate reality. As Peter encouraged those believers who

were homeless and persecuted: "But may the God of all grace, who called us to His eternal glory by Christ Jesus, after you have suffered a while, perfect, establish, strengthen, and settle you. To Him be the glory and the dominion forever and ever. Amen" (1 Peter 5:10–11).

My wife and I had the opportunity to travel to England and Scotland for two weeks with a small group. The trip was organized by a couple who had traveled to the United Kingdom many times and simply enjoyed sharing their experience with others at no financial gain. The trip was at cost, but the nine of us enjoyed the top-notch organization and arrangements. We hit typical spots in London, like the Tower of London and Churchill's War Room, but we also visited places like Olney, where John Newton and William Cowper composed their hymns, and Bedford, where John Bunyan wrote *Pilgrim's Progress*. The tour was rich in history and remarkable, as it included seeing the places and hearing the stories of Christ's saints of old, some who gave their lives for their faith.

In gathering a group to go on what they called a Christian Heritage tour, our host couple put together a prospectus, explaining costs, giving details, and mapping out the itinerary. So we knew what we were signing up for. Jesus gives us a prospectus of sorts for eternity future, which John records in his gospel account:

> Most assuredly, I say to you, the hour is coming, and now is, when the dead will hear the voice of the Son of God; and those who hear will live. For as the Father has life in Himself, so He has granted the Son to have life in Himself, and has given Him authority to execute judgment also, because He is the Son of Man. Do not marvel at this; for the hour is coming in which all who

are in the graves will hear His voice and come forth—
those who have done good, to the resurrection of life,
and those who have done evil, to the resurrection of
condemnation. (5:25–29)

Our England and Scotland trip was limited to those who
signed up. Jesus speaks of a trip every person will undertake,
heading for one of two destinations—life or condemnation.
How does one find a place in the resurrection of life? Our
Lord tells us in the prior verse: "Most assuredly, I say to you,
he who hears My word and believes in Him who sent Me has
everlasting life, and shall not come into judgment, but has
passed from death into life" (John 5:24). The life of which
Jesus speaks does not wait for the future but begins right
now for those who believe God's word and embrace His Son.
One day that life will come to full, unwilting, glorious bloom
in eternity.

My trip to the United Kingdom stretched over two
weeks. That seemed like a long time in some respects and not
enough in others. The experience was a delight. I didn't want
it to end. But being away from home takes its toll. Our life in
glory will be everlasting, and it will not take any toll because
we will be home. We grasp the glory of this eternal home by
seeing what it is not and what it is.

Life Not Death

Our Lord Jesus spoke of two resurrections in John 5:25–29,
which included two contrasting eternal states of being—life
and death—or to be more accurate, eternal life and eternal
death. Jesus tells us a parable about the last judgment. He
begins with this image: "When the Son of Man comes in
His glory, and all the holy angels with Him, then He will sit

on the throne of His glory. All the nations will be gathered before Him, and He will separate them one from another, as a shepherd divides his sheep from the goats" (Matt. 25:31–32). When Jesus returns, He will do so not in humility, as He did at his first coming, but in glory. When He came to endure the cross, Jesus did not come to judge. When He returns, it will be to judge. All those who have believed the Father and rested in Him by faith have already been judged and declared not guilty. Those who have rejected Christ will face judgment on their own merits. The first group Jesus calls sheep; the latter group, goats. To the sheep Jesus will say, "Then the King will say to those on His right hand, 'Come, you blessed of My Father, inherit the kingdom prepared for you from the foundation of the world'" (Matt. 25:34). To the goats, Christ on the throne of judgment will say, "Depart from Me, you cursed, into the everlasting fire prepared for the devil and his angels" (Matt. 25:41).

Jesus taught about hell. He spoke of "hell fire" (Matt. 5:22; 18:9). He explained a parable about the judgment to come:

> Then Jesus sent the multitude away and went into the house. And His disciples came to Him, saying, "Explain to us the parable of the tares of the field."
>
> He answered and said to them: "He who sows the good seed is the Son of Man. The field is the world, the good seeds are the sons of the kingdom, but the tares are the sons of the wicked one. The enemy who sowed them is the devil, the harvest is the end of the age, and the reapers are the angels. Therefore as the tares are gathered and burned in the fire, so it will be at the end of this age. The Son of Man will send out His angels, and they will gather out of His kingdom all things that offend, and those who practice lawlessness, and will

cast them into the furnace of fire. There will be wailing and gnashing of teeth. Then the righteous will shine forth as the sun in the kingdom of their Father. He who has ears to hear, let him hear!" (Matt. 13:36–43)

The letters of the New Testament also include teaching about hell and do so in sobering terms. For example, Paul writes this of those who reject the gospel of life found in Jesus Christ: "These shall be punished with everlasting destruction from the presence of the Lord and from the glory of His power" (2 Thess. 1:9; cf. John 3:36).

On our United Kingdom trip I had opportunity to visit St. Andrews, just north of Edinburgh, Scotland. We heard stories of godly men who gave their lives for the cause of Christ and the preservation of the gospel. We walked the grounds of the medieval castle ruins situated on a rocky outcropping overlooking the North Sea. It boasts a fascinating history, including a connection to John Knox, the Scottish Reformer.

What haunted me, though, from my visit to St. Andrews Castle was the dungeon. It's called the Bottle Dungeon because of its shape. The rock had been hollowed out in the shape of a laboratory flask, tapered at the top and flaring at the bottom. I peered into the opening to see the distant stone floor. I couldn't help but shiver as I imagined what it would be like to be thrown into it, as many prisoners were: no stairs, no ladder, no comforts, no escape, perhaps broken bones upon impact, and brutally cold. I can't imagine how desperate, how claustrophobic that would have been, accentuated by the shape that offered no purchase for freedom. That bottle dungeon represented to me sheer hopelessness and helplessness. Away from all comfort. An apt picture of the torment of hell.

In chapter 5 we considered Jesus's descent into hell. We pointed out that the hell in question was Hades or Sheol, making the point that Jesus really died and His soul was separated from His body, as is the case when any of us die. The hell of which Jesus warned, however, is not Hades but Gehenna, not a place of the departed but a place of punishment in satisfaction of divine justice in facing the unmitigated wrath of a holy God for those who refused to come to Christ and live.

It is against this backdrop of eternal death that the Apostles' Creed leads us to affirm resurrection to life everlasting for those whose faith is in Jesus Christ. By grace alone, through faith alone, in Christ alone our eternity is not death but life. But there is more to be said. Not only is life everlasting escape from the horrors of hell; not only is it life uncorrupted and uninterrupted by sin, sorrow, pain, death, or any other vestige of the fall—life everlasting promises something apart from which it would not be life at all.

This Is the Life

As I write this my son Nathan and his bride, Kate, are honeymooning in Punta Cana. He texted me a picture of them at their resort enjoying their first meal, delivered right to their room that looked out on the sapphire-blue Caribbean Sea. They had in store a week of pampering, leisure, and adventure. I can hear them breathing a deep sigh of delight and saying, "This is the life." Even as wonderful as that sounds, it is insufficient as a picture of the joys of eternal life. The everlasting life that we declare in the Creed is not perpetual vacation. It is the experience of a world uninfected, unaffected by sin's curse. It is life free from sin—its effects, power, and consequences. We are so steeped in a fallen creation existence, it's hard for us to imagine. The book of Revelation gives us extraordinary pictures of streets of gold and gates of pearl to communicate awe and beauty. But even these pictures are inadequate to convey the glory of what is yet to come. The book use images and analogies to give us some sense of what God has in store for those who love Him.

Yet the greatest glory that awaits us is not a pain-free existence. Rather, our greatest delight will be uninterrupted, unimpeded communion with our Lord. The latter part of the book of Revelation uses the imagery of a bride and groom to give us a sense of the wonder of eternal life:

> And I heard, as it were, the voice of a great multi-tude, as the sound of many waters and as the sound of mighty thunderings, saying, "Alleluia! For the Lord God Omnipotent reigns! Let us be glad and rejoice and give Him glory, for the marriage of the Lamb has come, and His wife has made herself ready." And to her it was granted to be arrayed in fine linen, clean and bright, for the fine linen is the righteous acts of the saints.
>
> Then he said to me, "Write: 'Blessed are those who are called to the marriage supper of the Lamb!'" And he said to me, "These are the true sayings of God." (Rev. 19:6–9)

Sometimes when we think of marriage, our minds go to the bliss but also to conflicts that must be settled by for-giveness and submission to one another in the Lord. The metaphor of marriage in the book of Revelation, however, is intended to communicate love and intimacy. It speaks to the grace of God to make those not loved and unlovable loved with an everlasting love (see Hos. 1:2–10 and 1 Peter 2:9–10).

Unlike with Nathan and Kate, there will be no honeymoon period followed by the struggles of real life because real life will be sin-free.

Peter tells us how the joy of life everlasting breaks through the afflictions of life now. That joy is not just in relief from suffering but in love for our Beloved, "whom having not seen you love. Though now you do not see Him, yet believing, you rejoice with joy inexpressible and full of glory, receiving the end of your faith—the salvation of your souls" (1 Peter 1:8–9).

Through faith now we behold Christ and we love Him. But faith will give way to sight, and we will behold Him face-to-face. Jesus put eternal life in these terms: "And this is eternal life, that they may know You, the only true God, and Jesus Christ whom You have sent" (John 17:3). The zenith of eternal life is fully enjoying our God into all eternity and experiencing a love for Him that cannot be fathomed. Paul's prayer for the Ephesians will be finally be answered: "that He would grant you, according to the riches of His glory, to be strengthened with might through His Spirit in the inner man, that Christ may dwell in your hearts through faith; that you, being rooted and grounded in love, may be able to comprehend with all the saints what is the width and length and depth and height—to know the love of Christ which passes knowledge; that you may be filled with all the fullness of God" (Eph. 3:16–19).

Intimacy with Jesus by knowing Him, being with Him in unbroken, unimpeded, unfiltered communion—this is the glory of eternal life, for which we will have an insatiable appetite and infinite repast. Prior to going to the garden of Gethsemane, where He would be betrayed, and then suffering under Pontius Pilate and sentenced to crucifixion, Jesus spent time with His disciples, celebrating His final Passover. He comforted them with these words: "Let not your heart be troubled; you believe in God, believe also in Me. In My Father's house are many mansions; if it were not so, I would have told you. I go to prepare a place for you. And if I go and prepare a place for you, I will come again and receive you to Myself; that where I am, there you may be also" (John 14:1–3). When we think of a mansion, our minds go to something big and sprawling. A few years ago my wife and I stayed at a bed and breakfast in Newport, Rhode Island. Part of our time included touring a few of the mansions there. These massive summer residences, called cottages by their uber-wealthy owners, were built in the Gilded Age, prior to the enactment of income tax. The opulence was astounding. These mansions were not built in a housing development but on spacious grounds with plenty of privacy. Some mansions we see are gated, accessed by a long, winding driveway cutting through manicured lawns and exquisitely landscaped grounds to the door of a palatial home. The term *mansion* communicates an individual, spacious, luxurious residence.

But that is nothing like what Jesus wants us to envision. He has in mind a dwelling, where we live into eternity. The word for *mansion* can simply be put "home." Later in the chapter Jesus uses the same word, this time translated "home": "Jesus answered and said to him, 'If anyone loves Me, he will keep My word; and My Father will love him, and We will come to him and make Our home with him'" (John 14:23). When Jesus extends to us the comfort of mansions, He is not suggesting we will each have our own Newport mansion. Rather, He is promising us that we will be at home with

Him forever. The "many" dwellings speaks not to isolation but to inclusion, expressive of the communion of saints who together will share in God's blessings and Christ's joy and glory (John 17:24).

Sounds like a fairy tale, doesn't it? Live happily ever after. But it's not. Fairy tales are not real. This is our Father's tale, the tale of God the Father almighty, Maker of heaven and earth, Maker of the new heaven and the new earth. Rather than transient happiness, we will enter into the joy of our Master. The Apostles' Creed begins by lifting our eyes to the eternal Creator God. It keeps our gaze there throughout the giving of His Son and sending of His Spirit. It ends by lifting our gaze to the horizon of history, when we who belong to Christ, as Paul puts it, "shall always be with the Lord" (1 Thess. 4:17).

Conclusion
AMEN

Earlier I mentioned an ornate plaque I had seen at a church in London. It was situated at the front of a room where people gathered for worship. On it was the text of the Apostles' Creed in simple type, starting with "in God the Father almighty." Above that simple type were the words "I believe" in fancy script about ten times the size of the font of the body of the Creed. Under the text was the word "amen," also in fancy script and the same size as "I believe." Why such prominence for such a seemingly inconsequential word as amen?

The word *amen* means "so be it." When we say amen at the close of our prayers, we add a note of authenticity and affirmation to what we have said. When others join us in saying amen, they align themselves with what we have prayed. Amen is not a way to say "the end" but a way to convey consent. To say amen to the Creed is to affirm its declarations. It is more than a period; it gives the exclamation point to "I believe." For as detailed as our opening chapter was on "I believe," this final chapter on *amen* is brief. The reason is that it repeats all that was involved in belief and reinforces the statements of faith that followed. Amen functions as a bookend of belief.

Amen reinforces faith with acknowledgment, affirmation, and agreement. It says that my faith is saving faith, not merely having information or even approving the facts are real and true but saying, "I rest; I trust," for my salvation. The declarations of the Apostles' Creed are mine as a Christian. They are ours as Christians.

Some parts of the contemporary church don't recite creeds. But reciting the Apostles' Creed joins our voices with God's people over the centuries in proclaiming the gospel of salvation. Let me close with a story that emphasizes the importance of creeds in the life of the church. I can't remember where I heard it, but its impact stuck with me.

A young pastor was asked to visit a dying man in a Washington, DC, hospital. The man was dying of aggressive bone cancer. Of his own admission, he was not a Christian. The pastor shared the gospel with him; the man wasn't particularly interested. But the pastor continued to visit, and a friendship formed. He got to know the dying man. The man had grown up in Spain. His mother had taught him the Christian faith, but he had rejected it when his father was killed.

The man came to America. He worked hard. He went to college and on to medical school. He became a highly respected physician. Then came the cancer. His body that he kept in shape started to deteriorate. His skills diminished to such a degree he had to stop his medical practice. All the accomplishments and many accolades of his lifetime became empty. He became empty. He said to the young pastor, "What can your God possibly do for me?"

The pastor explained the gospel again. He pointed him to what Jesus did and the forgiveness and hope found in Jesus. The man didn't interact. The visit ended.

A few days later, the man's leg broke spontaneously from the cancer. The doctors had to operate. The night before the operation, the man wrote a note. It was for the pastor, and it was partly in Spanish. The part in Spanish was the words to the Apostles' Creed because that's how the man had memorized it as a kid. His note continued in English: "Jesus, I hate all my sins. I have not served or worshiped you. Father, I know the only way to come into your kingdom is by the precious blood of Jesus. I know you stand at the door and you will answer those who knock. I want to be your lamb." By God's grace he embraced the faith of the Apostles' Creed as his own. That man didn't survive the operation, but he did survive his death.

Think now of a worship service. Believers are gathered as Christ's church, the communion of saints, for the purpose of the praise of God's glory. The pastor prompts the people, "Christian, what do you believe?" The chorus of voices from the congregation does not erupt in a cacophony of different beliefs but in a symphony of gospel truth, confessing the apostolic faith. All God's promises are yes and amen in Jesus Christ. The congregation joins in the great amen, and God is glorified. To borrow the words of the hymn:

> Praise to the Lord!
>> Oh let all that is in me adore Him!
> All that hath life and breath,
>> come now with praises before Him!

Let the Amen sound from His people again;
Gladly for aye we adore Him.[1]

Forever!

---

1. Joachim Neander, "Praise to the Lord, the Almighty," in the public domain.